Edinburgh Waverley

A Novel Railway Station

Ann Glen

 NetworkRail

Previous page: A portion of the extensive train shed roof at
Edinburgh Waverley with its shallow lattice girders of steel, rods for
wind strengthening and tall cast iron columns for support. (Ann Glen)

First published in the
Isle of Man in 2013 by
Lily Publications Ltd
PO Box 33
Ramsey
Isle of Man IM99 4LP

Contents

The facade of Waverley Station from the east. (Ann Glen)

Foreword

The most remarkable realisation about the history of Waverley Station is the extent to which decisions made hundreds of years ago still have daily implications on the lives of the capital's 21st century passengers.

The railway was always regarded as a bit of an unsightly necessity by Victorian Edinburgh's New Town elite. For that very reason, it was hidden from view, channelled through a tunnel from Haymarket and into the natural valley between the castle rock and Princes Street. The natural screening meant that steam trains wouldn't be visible through the windows of up market Georgian town houses.

The same distaste for industrial landmarks meant that the city's most central station was also required to hide itself from view. Rather than build a station which was designed to celebrate this technological transportation marvel like many major British industrial cities, Edinburgh chose to disguise its station in the ancient Nor Loch valley. This location, at the lowest point of the city centre has meant that heavy rainfall has always presented the station with challenges. Only in recent years has the flooding risk in Princes Street Gardens been substantially reduced, while one of the unseen recent improvements at the station has been vastly improved drainage.

Ann Glen's enlightening documentation of the station's evolution shows how the rail operators of years gone by tried to tackle these geographic restrictions, how the station gradually established an identity of its own and how the challenges faced by railwaymen 180 years ago still resonate now.

The natural restrictions imposed by the station's location will always present challenges for operators. When the Forth Bridge opened in 1890, railway operators were eventually forced to create another tunnel to Haymarket to increase capacity to the west of the station. Similar innovation was required last decade as demand for rail travel rocketed during the early 21st century. Rather than more tunnels, Network Rail boosted the number of trains using Waverley by improving the flexibility of the track layout, lengthening station platforms and electrifying more routes.

In 2013, more trains and more passengers use the station than ever before, however, the topography of the station hasn't improved and its location in a valley has always presented an issue for people entering and leaving. While the ramps continue to offer a steep incline up to Waverley Bridge, the expectations of modern passengers have also resulted in improved step-free access to Princes Street, Market Street and Calton Road.

By far the most obvious improvement to Waverley in 2013 is the crystal clear glazed roof which has now been revealed after several years of being shrouded by its scaffold cocoon. The roof had never been renewed in its entirety since it was first built to shelter Waverley's long suffering passengers at the end of the 19th century and by 2010, it showed.

The new canopy once again establishes a sense of grandeur for a station which has had its fair share of unflattering changes and additions. The achievement in managing such a major refurbishment while millions of passengers carried on, business as usual, below the decking should not be underestimated. It has been a triumph for the project teams and their contractors as much as it has been an extraordinary feat for the station operations team, helping passengers find their platforms through a maze of hoardings.

Even now, as we reflect on the incredible difference these refurbishment works have made, the history of the station teaches us that the next metamorphosis cannot be far off. The recent transformations of London's St Pancras and Kings Cross have set new benchmarks for Britain's railways and have shown us the importance of offering passengers an improved journey from end to end.

Waverley will always be enveloped by Edinburgh's historic city centre but hidden under its newly gleaming canopy is a thrumming transport hub which keeps the capital's heart beating. It might be located in Edinburgh's geographic 'gutter', but Waverley is reaching for the stars.

David Simpson, July 2013
Route Managing Director, Scotland
Network Rail

Introduction

Edinburgh Waverley is unique. It sits in the midst of a World Heritage Site and it is the second largest railway station in the British Isles. Yet it has an unassuming presence – it is no cathedral of the railways – but has been cleverly designed by Victorian engineers to make intelligent use of a difficult location. Strategically situated between the Old Town on the tail of the castle crag and the New Town on easier ground to the north, it lies in a trench where the land was gouged away by ice sheets and melt waters some 12,000 years ago.

Waverley is not just a place of arrivals and departures, it has also been a setting for rendezvous, romance and even mystery. Most of the day, it is thronged with passengers and echoes to their footfall and conversations. Trains rumble in and out, announcements resonate and the big information board buzzes. In 'the wee sma' hours', the station is deserted and strangely quiet – unless engineers have a possession on a line for maintenance. By morning, Waverley's tempo quickens from a trickle of passengers to a flood as the rush hours approach.

With its many platforms offering destinations in a multitude of directions, Waverley is a market hall for rail travel. With a throughput of some 23.5 million passengers a year, it is one of the busiest stations in Britain and the number keeps growing. It introduces thousands of visitors to the capital of Scotland and to a city that is also a renowned festival venue, facts reflected in the busy summer months for the railway. Situated in the centre of the city it has served for over 170 years, 'The Waverley', occupies a special place in the hearts of Edinburgh citizens and many others worldwide.

The main concourse (formerly the west concourse) at Edinburgh Waverley. (Ann Glen)

The Scott Monument (left) in Princes Street Gardens and Waverley Bridge (right) with Waverley Station's west platforms (centre). (Ann Glen)

What's in a Name?

The name itself is intriguing and comes from the novels of Sir Walter Scott (1777-1832) who was born in Edinburgh and educated at the Royal High School. He found fame from writing historical novels, epic poems and plays. Although now rather out of fashion in literary circles, Sir Walter won international acclaim in his lifetime. He trained as a lawyer and became closely associated with the Scottish Borders as Sheriff of Selkirkshire. As a youth recovering from illness, he first heard tales of adventure in the 'South Country' that became the inspiration for many of his books and poems. Through their 'romantic appeal', Walter Scott is credited with 'kick starting' tourism in Scotland as the better off flocked to see the places associated with his writings.

'Waverley', Scott's first novel, was published anonymously in 1814. However, intelligent guesswork soon narrowed down the question of authorship and in 1827 this was revealed to be Sir Walter. 'Waverley' is the name of the story's hero and is said to come from Waverley Abbey in Surrey, a 12th century monastic establishment beside the River Wey. It has been suggested that Sir Walter visited the area in the early 1800s and justified the choice of the name 'Waverley' as *'an uncontaminated name, bearing with its sound little of good or evil, excepting what the reader shall hereafter be pleased to affix to it'.* Sir Walter had a wide antiquarian interest and the abbey, ruinous since the 1560s, may well have attracted his attention. The site is now in the care of English Heritage. Incidentally, the word 'Waverley' is Old English and means the meadow of the aspen tree.

With such world renown, it was inevitable that one of Edinburgh's most distinguished sons would be commemorated with a noble memorial. The Scott Monument on Princes Street was begun in 1841 when an Act of Parliament was obtained for the purpose. Completed in 1844 and inaugurated two years later, this Victorian Gothic tower still bares the grime of 'Auld Reekie', Scott's name for the once smoky city.

By 1846, the term 'Waverley Bridge' was being applied by the Ordnance Survey to the masonry bridge giving access to the monument site from the south. The bridge crossed the new lines of the Edinburgh & Glasgow Railway at the Little Mound and a railway station was developed close by. Soon

Sir Walter Scott from whose first novel 'Waverley' the railway station takes its name. (Wikipedia)

'the station at Waverley Bridge' became 'Waverley Station'.

When British Railways closed Princes Street Station, the city's other railway terminus, on 18 April 1966, Waverley was renamed just 'Edinburgh'. Concerned citizens saw this as an affront to their historic railway station – the public would have none of it. A petition was begun by a local newsagent and soon attracted over 5,000 signatures. Faced with such 'grass roots' protest, the name 'Waverley' was officially reinstated.

How Edinburgh's railways began

In the early eighteenth century, wheeled vehicles were rolling along the tracks of the Tranent & Cockenzie Waggonway east of Edinburgh. It arose from a property acquisition after the 1715 Jacobite Rising when the Scottish estates of many of the supporters of the Stuart dynasty were confiscated and so the coalmines of Tranent came into the ownership of the York Buildings Company. This was an English speculation that constructed a wooden-railed waggonway some 2½ miles long conveying coal for export to a harbour at Cockenzie on the Firth of Forth. This is judged to be Scotland's earliest railway. The track was 3ft 3in gauge and being downhill was worked by gravity. Even so, a large embankment, which still stands, was necessary near the village of Tranent. Horses were only used to bring the empty waggons back to the pits.

Strangely, the waggonway was implicated in the Jacobite Rising of 1745 when government cannon were placed on the track formation at the battle of Prestonpans.

By the 1800s Walter Scott would have been acquainted with the various proposals to improve the transport connections to and from Edinburgh. The city was desperately short of fuel. To supply Edinburgh's many fireplaces in homes and industries, coal – and plenty of it – was essential. In the early 1800s, there was an interest in building a canal from the city to connect with the Forth & Clyde Canal near Falkirk and thereby have the potential to serve both Edinburgh and Leith. Robert Stevenson, the engineer to the Commissioners of the Northern Lighthouses and of Bell Rock fame, made a survey in 1814 and later presented a report to Edinburgh Town Council.

Neither the marshy Nor Loch site nor the 'Earthen Mound', formed of spoil from the New Town, were seen as insuperable obstacles for the canal whose main purpose would be to supply the city with coal. Indeed, it was argued that lateral cuts and 'rail-roads' could be made to 'all the coal-fields within ten miles' of the waterway. Stevenson suggested forming a basin – where Waverley Station would later be sited – with the canal continuing under the old North Bridge by way of Abbeyhill and so to Leith. The passage downhill would have required fourteen locks but the merchants of Leith opposed

Upper left: A gateway leading to the on the track bed of the Tranent & Cockenzie Waggonway of 1733, Scotland's first railway. Lower left: A stone sleeper from the Waggonway in a roadside wall. Above right: The coal-stained shores of Cockenzie harbour, the terminus of the Tranent & Cockenzie Waggonway. (all Ann Glen)

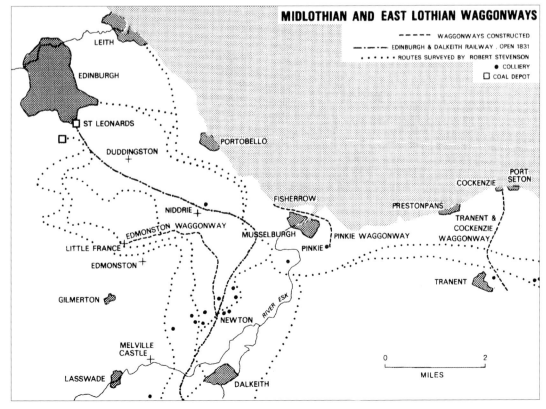

- - - - - WAGGONWAYS CONSTRUCTED
-·-·-·- EDINBURGH & DALKEITH RAILWAY . OPEN 1831
· · · · · ROUTES SURVEYED BY ROBERT STEVENSON
● COLLIERY
□ COAL DEPOT

LEITH

EDINBURGH

ST LEONARDS

PORTOBELLO

DUDDINGSTON

FISHERROW

NIDDRIE

EDMONSTON WAGGONWAY

MUSSELBURGH

PINKIE WAGGONWAY

LITTLE FRANCE

PINKIE

EDMONSTON

COCKENZIE

PORT SETON

PRESTONPANS

TRANENT & COCKENZIE WAGGONWAY

TRANENT

GILMERTON

RIVER ESK

NEWTON

MELVILLE CASTLE

LASSWADE

DALKEITH

0   2

MILES

The painting (above) by Alexander Nasmyth of the view from Princes Street to the old North Bridge in 1825 shows the site of the residual Nor Loch and the location where Waverley Station would arise. The Royal Scottish Institution (now the Royal Scottish Academy) is under construction (right) on the Mound.
(National Galleries of Scotland)

Left: The extensive system of waggonways that developed east of Edinburgh.
(C.J.A. Robertson)

A horse-drawn chaldron wagon took up to 3 tons of coal. (Scottish Mining Museum)

the canal because it would cut through their golf links right beside the clubhouse, and it was never constructed.

Also dating from 1814 was the Pinkie Railway, a waggonway just 1¾ miles long near Musselburgh taking coal to the small harbour at Fisherrow. In Newton parish, south east of Edinburgh where many coal pits were sunk, another 'rail-road' was laid. The versatile Robert Stevenson was the engineer for the Edmonstone or Newton Railway, a 4 mile long line that used edge rails. Opened in 1818 it fed a depot at Little France, thereby reducing the distance for cartage on the poor roads leading to the city.

Eventually the Union Canal, linking Edinburgh to the Forth & Clyde Canal near Falkirk, was opened in 1822. However,

it only reached basins and wharves at the west end of the city – nowadays the Lochrin Basin is the sole survivor. Canal barges could then carry coal supplies from the Monklands of Lanarkshire to the city. Meanwhile, collier vessels from Northumbria continued to bring their cargoes to Leith. But there was a downside – just when demand was greatest in winter, these waterborne supplies could be much delayed when the canals froze or sea trade was storm bound.

However, there was plenty of coal in the Lothians though distribution to the city was difficult. In September 1824, a meeting was called in a city coffee house 'to consider building a railway from the Lothian coalfield to the city'. The idea had been aired earlier when Robert Stevenson had surveyed a route but the attitude of influential landed proprietors, the coal lords – Buccleuch, Lothian and Rosebery – had been negative. They were now persuaded to support the scheme.

That same year, editorials in 'The Scotsman' advocated a comprehensive system of Scottish railways – all on the same gauge and hauled by steam locomotives. 'The Glasgow Herald' also stated:-

'Although the locomotive engine is a late invention and not generally understood, it seems to be nearly perfect in construction, and it is efficient almost beyond belief in operation'. 5 November 1824

By the autumn of 1825, George Stephenson's 'Locomotion' was hauling both goods and passengers on the

The former level crossing on the Edinburgh & Dalkeith Railway at Duddingston is now part of National Cycle Route 1. (Ewan Crawford)

Stockton & Darlington Railway – the first line to be built by public subscription. Furthermore, railway construction was proving only one-third of the cost of canals.

Plans had been prepared for a waggonway on the 4ft 6in Scotch gauge for coal haulage, and in May 1826 an Act for the Edinburgh & Dalkeith Railway (E&DR) was obtained. The engineer was James Jardine, Dumfries-shire born and a graduate of Edinburgh University who had expertise in geology and mathematics. A depot was set up at St Leonards on the city's southern margin below Salisbury Crags from where the tracks went down a 572 yard long tunnel at a slope of 1 in 30. This was the first on any Scottish railway. It was worked by an inclined plane involving two stationary steam engines at the top and was gas lit.

The E&DR was double tracked from the outset and horse-hauled throughout its existence. Opened to the nearest coal pit on 4 July 1831, it was eventually a system of almost 14 miles; its tracks continued east by Duddingston Loch, Niddrie, Millerhill and Hardengreen to Dalhousie (Newtongrange). Near there it met the Marquis of Lothian's Waggonway on an alignment that the revived Borders Railway will now follow. Jardine designed dramatic viaducts to cross the deep valleys of the North and South Esk. (In addition, he constructed several reservoirs for Edinburgh's water supply and was the first to determine 'mean sea level', a measurement essential in cartography and surveying).

Soon further branches of the E&DR were extended to Fisherrow's harbour on the Forth and to South Leith. The lines brought prosperity to local landowners through the efficient carriage of coal and farm produce to and from St Leonards depot – it boasted a weighbridge, then an innovation. In June 1832 a passenger service began using a converted stagecoach and the E&DR soon attracted thousands of passengers to enjoy leisurely jaunts through the Lothian countryside. Such excursions were relaxed affairs. A byelaw forbade drivers from allowing their horses to graze while hauling trains, and it was reported that tickets were not much used 'as passengers would not tell, or had not made up their minds as to where they were going'. The E&DR achieved fame as the 'Innocent Railway', a line of

'indestructive character', without mishaps, in which the public could have confidence. Rustic though it was, it gave Edinburgh people a taste for travel by rail.

Within a decade, the days of the waggonways were numbered and Parliamentary powers were enabling the first main lines to be constructed to the city. These would be of standard gauge at 4ft 8½in with trains hauled by steam locomotives. The origins of Waverley Station were set to begin.

Top left: This tunnel on the Edinburgh & Dalkeith Railway was the first on any line in Scotland. (John Peter)
Top right: The cycle path on the track bed of the Edinburgh & Dalkeith Railway. (Ann Glen)
Above: The Glenesk viaduct once carried a waggonway for coal traffic in the Lothians and will be part of the Borders Railway. (Network Rail)

How Waverley Station began

The Railway Age was dawning in Scotland and the desirability of an inter-city railway connecting the historic capital of Edinburgh with the commercial metropolis of Glasgow was soon being debated. After the Liverpool & Manchester Railway was opened to acclaim in the autumn of 1830, the idea of trunk routes linking major cities came to the fore. Engineering expertise was growing and business partnerships were being formed – the firm of Grainger & Miller was one. By 1824 Thomas Grainger of Edinburgh was the engineer and surveyor to the Monkland & Kirkintilloch Railway. He had considerable experience in road works, a skill transferable to track beds for railways, while his partner John Miller from Ayr was an indefatigable young man who

had forsaken the law for mathematics. For several decades, this partnership was to be pre-eminent in the civil engineering of Scottish railways.

The actual route that an inter-city railway across the Central Lowlands might take had been considered intermittently; James Jardine had surveyed a line in 1825-26 through Tollcross, Bellshill and Shotts. The Liverpool & Manchester Railway's success gave fresh impetus to the notion of tracks connecting the two cities and including the port of Leith. A railway between Edinburgh and Glasgow was a tempting possibility for Grainger & Miller. To give the line a head start in the west, they proposed using the Garnkirk & Glasgow Railway, which they had also engineered.

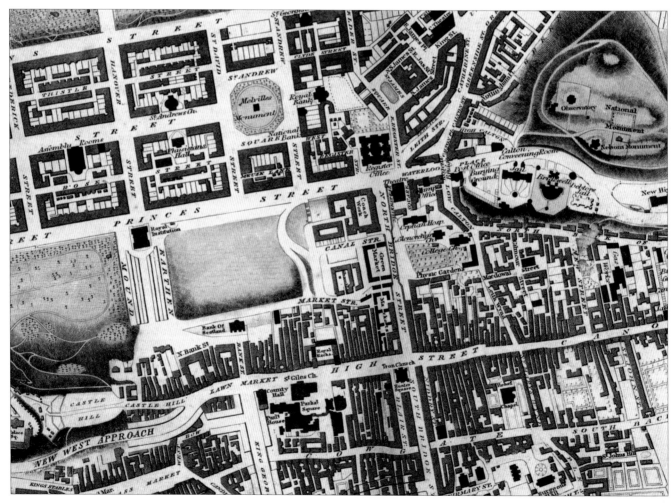

James Kay's Plan of Edinburgh in 1836 shows the central location where Waverley Station would be built – between Market Street (south) and Canal Street (north) with the North Bridge, historic churches and Physic Garden on the east. (National Library of Scotland)

By December 1830 Grainger & Miller had drawn up a report on the 'Edinburgh, Glasgow & Leith Railway' in which John Miller took the lead. George Stephenson, the renowned engineer, was asked to review the two possible routes. He held a radical view believing that the principal purpose of the railway should be 'the expeditious, safe and cheap conveyance of passengers' which for Scotland was remarkable as Scots saw railways as freight carriers, subservient to canals and harbours. Stephenson preferred the Grainger & Miller route as its summit levels were lower, but the arguments were in vain – in 1832 the Bill was thrown out by Parliament at Westminster.

Nevertheless, the demand for travel and for trade was growing. In 1835 a meeting was called to discuss possible improvements in transport between Edinburgh, the port of Leith and the many small harbours on the shores of the Forth from which ferries, sailing and steam packets plied. The outcome was an Act of 13 August 1836 for the Edinburgh, Leith & Newhaven Railway from Princes Street to Newhaven with a branch to serve Leith. Short though this would be, it was a radical proposal calling for a tunnel under the New Town. The name 'Canal Street' was an echo from the

Above left: John Miller, CE, FRSE, the distinguished engineer to the Edinburgh & Glasgow Railway and many other Scottish lines. (GSWRA/Roland Paxton)

Above: Granton Harbour from which ferries plied across the Forth in connection with trains from Canal Street Station. (Ian Smith Collection)

Stevenson plan of 1814 but this time would be used for a railway station. With expensive land ownership and engineering issues to be confronted, this line's viability was soon being questioned.

Before the Edinburgh, Leith & Newhaven line was even completed, the Duke of Buccleuch, a major landowner, determined on having a better harbour at Granton. That port's ferry shuttles across the Forth became a focus for goods traffic and the railway was subsequently renamed the Edinburgh, Leith & Granton. A revised plan in 1839 took the line to Trinity but the controversial tunnel from Canal Street remained. In fact, there was more than one tunnel on the

An engineering triumph that dates from 1842 is the thirty-six arch Almond valley viaduct constructed on the Edinburgh & Glasgow Railway. (Ann Glen)

This rear view of Haymarket Station will be concealed by the new station being built on the adjacent site. (Ann Glen)

route making the civil engineering demanding and expensive.

On 4 July 1838, at the third attempt, an Act was obtained for the Edinburgh & Glasgow Railway to provide a direct route between the cities. Grainger & Miller planned it as a high speed trunk line of standard gauge, although 5ft 6in with stone sleepers had been considered. Valleys were crossed by imposing structures such as the thirty-six arch Almond Valley viaduct and major tunnels were formed at Falkirk, Winchburgh and Glasgow. The mile long rock cutting at Croy was the most daunting of several on the way. Although the line closely followed the routes of the canals of earlier date, its superb engineering is a testimony to Miller's surveying and design skills. The outcome was a remarkably level alignment from Haymarket to Cowlairs but the severe incline of 1 in 41 in the tunnel giving access to Dundas Street station, (later renamed Queen Street) in Glasgow was to prove not only dangerous but also time wasting.

The Edinburgh & Glasgow opened on 18 February 1842 to Haymarket, west of central Edinburgh. Separate dinners were held for the elites in both cities as they had not been unanimous in their support for the project. The E&G marked a new era in the social and economic history of the two cities by bringing 'ease and convenience' to travel. There were four trains each way per day taking on average 2½ hours, a welcome improvement as the best stagecoaches had taken four. First Class was 8s (40p) but the 6am luggage train was only 2s6d (12.5p). The E&G, as it is still known in railway circles, was phenomenally successful and Third Class was especially popular even although passengers stood in open trucks without roofs or windows.

The Edinburgh & Glasgow stations were said to be uncomfortable and chaotic – hardly a positive introduction to railway travel. Yet rail was emerging as a remarkably safe form of passenger transport and the E&G had fixed signals

Haymarket Station, in neo-classical style, dates from 1842 when the Edinburgh & Glasgow Railway opened. (Ann Glen)

and the electric telegraph from the outset. It brought new opportunities as for the first time, people could visit places of which they had only heard – for Edinburgh folk, the Firth of Clyde with its steamers and the Burns Country became favourite excursions. As early as August 1845, a 'pleasure excursion to Loch Long & Loch Lomond' was being advertised. However, such trains were not always welcome in rural areas as they brought 'the idleness and dissipation of the city…to pour it upon peaceful hamlets'.

Ever enterprising, the E&G was also prepared to run Sunday trains at a time when religious controversy raged in Scotland. The company's contract with the Royal Mail obliged it to run mail trains on Sundays. Many considered such journeys sinful and confrontations at stations in support of Sabbatarian principles continued for years. Others thought Sunday trains as 'means of mercy and necessity' might just be permissible.

The terminus and headquarters of the Edinburgh & Glasgow were located at Haymarket where the original sandstone building continues in use. (In 1982 when the adjacent timber train shed with its cast iron columns was removed to make space for a car park, the structure found a new home at the Bo'ness & Kinneil Railway). The E&G soon had sidings for coal distribution adjacent to its station and an engine shed erected a little further west.

The Edinburgh & Glasgow saw its station at Haymarket as a temporary solution – it wished to take its line into central Edinburgh, a proposal strenuously opposed by the property owners facing Princes Street Gardens. An Act of 1816 had given them the right to prevent commercial development and to preserve their unobstructed vista to the pleasure gardens and Edinburgh Castle. Not for the first time would railway interests be at variance with the Princes Street proprietors who feared a serious loss of amenity and a fall in property values. The residents, led by Lord Cockburn, a High Court judge and pioneering conservationist, resolutely defended their environment. He forecast that bringing the E&G through the valley would ruin it:-

'the whole beautiful ground will be given up to railways, with their yards, depots, counting houses, and other abominations, at least on the east side…'

Meantime, the Haymarket terminus was saving the E&G costs that would arise from having to tunnel eastwards through a projection of volcanic rock, part of the Castle crag.

In August 1842 the Edinburgh, Leith & Granton Railway had opened its short section from Scotland Street to Trinity; however, its terminus at Canonmills was cramped and awkward while Scotland Street was inconvenient for the city centre. Nevertheless, by the summer of 1846 its rails had reached the ports of both Granton and Leith and tapped into the trade of these harbours.

Meanwhile, the North British Railway (NBR), a company that was to feature on the Scottish railway scene for almost

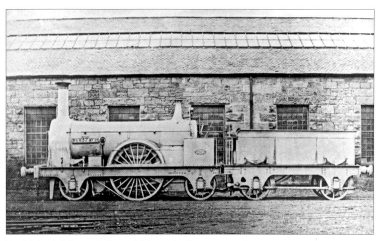

This Edinburgh & Glasgow Railway 2-2-2 locomotive No. 57 is a type that ran express services between the cities in the early 1850s. (J.L. Stevenson Collection)

80 years, had also been launched in 1842. It was a progeny of the Edinburgh & Glasgow, and grew to be Scotland's largest rail network. A meeting was held on 8 January that year in the E&G offices at Haymarket station with a view to promoting a thirty-mile long railway from Edinburgh to Dunbar over the coastal plain. It was envisaged that such a route would soon extend south to Berwick-on-Tweed to meet with English lines coming towards the Scottish Border. A great trunk line up the east coast would inevitably result. (In fact, there had been plans for a 'Great North British Railway from Edinburgh to Newcastle via Berwick' in 1839). However, there was a problem – not enough money to construct such a line was forthcoming in Scotland. The original prospectus of the NBR stated its intention 'to avoid all useless expense in ornamental works at stations or otherwise' – its Edinburgh terminus would be plain, cramped and uninspiring, outcomes which it would find hard to shake off.

The mid-1840s were momentous for railway development in Britain as people realised just how profitable railways could be. Railways were helping to expand economic activity – indeed, they were becoming major industries in their own right. Middle class money from factories and mills, especially

A view towards Calton Hill shows the market that lay under the old North Bridge on land that would become railway property. (Ian Smith Collection)

in Lancashire, was available for investment. Government bonds once thought 'safe' now seemed much less rewarding than railway stock. So investors were eager to put their money into railway companies and 'Railway Mania' took a grip. Numerous companies were promoted and Acts of Parliament sought. (Grainger & Miller themselves deposited Parliamentary Plans for over 1,500 miles of railway in this phase and some consulting engineers specialised in promoting or opposing Railway Bills).

Many Scottish schemes were advertised each accompanied by a prospectus setting out potential returns in glowing terms. Investors pored over newspaper reports and such journals as the *Scottish Railway Gazette* searching for hot tips while stocks and shares in railway companies were traded at silly prices. Proposals for trunk lines came to typify the boom years and the name of George Hudson, a Yorkshire entrepreneur, came to the fore. By amalgamations and take-overs, this 'Railway King' soon controlled tracks opening out from York through the Midlands. Indeed, he was a founding father of the Midland Railway Company in 1844. Claiming influence over 1,500 miles of line and £30 millions in capital, Hudson drove forward the east coast route to Scotland. His advice was sought by the NBR and he suggested that Lancashire money might be tapped. This was done and the line was duly authorised on 4 July 1844. However, its English shareholder majority was to call the tune for many years to come and Hudson himself cast eyes on the NBR. (It was not unusual for Scotland to be referred to as 'North Britain' at the time, with 'N.B.' appearing on aristocrats' and business letterheads).

The North British Railway established itself at the North Bridge, an eleven arch structure that had straddled the valley between the Old Town and the New Town since 1772. Just east of its north arch stood Lady Glenorchy's Chapel or North Church. This wealthy patroness of evangelical missions had supported its building in the 1770s. The plain lofty stone hall stood in the way of the NBR lines and so was removed in 1845. The acquisitions continued – land earmarked for

The old North Bridge with the stances for the 'green market' in fruit and vegetables that found shelter beneath it. (Ian Smith Collection)

public baths at Low Calton, a house in St.Andrew's Square for offices, and a brewery site at Meadowbank for an engine shed, subsequently known as St Margaret's.

By February of the following year, 'Plans and Elevations of Station at Edinburgh' were laid before the directors. These were approved and sent to the Magistrates and Town Council for inspection. The pace was quickening – a passenger manager was appointed at £200 and three clerks at £80 to £50 per annum. Patterns of tickets were investigated, a Glasgow printer making a better offer than 'Mr Edmonston', the established supplier to railways. Engine, carriage and goods sheds – all temporary structures – were approved and 280 goods vehicles were ordered. In October, a joint Edinburgh station with the E&G was under consideration but the NBR baulked at making a contribution of £10,000 towards it.

A vegetable or 'green' market used the North Bridge for shelter. It was a 'twilight zone' close to the back slope of the Old Town. The NBR put a wall round the market area and, taking an arch for its tracks, named its station 'North Bridge'. For the rail exit eastwards, a 398yd tunnel had to be driven through Calton Hill. Its 1 in 78 gradient was uphill to the station – indeed, this would be the steepest place on the entire East Coast main line and was not an easy place for incoming trains. It was also difficult for trains setting off as brakes were rudimentary. Nevertheless, the E&G's convergence with the NBR was inspected by Major-General Pasley, Inspector General of Railways on behalf of the Board of Trade. He reported that the extension had two lines of rails, laid complete throughout its length, and that both companies had sidings near their junction at the North Bridge. (In reality, the junction between the two was at the City Weigh House in Canal Street).

Nevertheless, North Bridge Station was opened with due ceremony on 18 June 1846 when a train of fifty carriages hauled by nine locomotives conveyed notables to Berwick-on-Tweed. After this impressive display, public services began to Berwick and trains were also advertised over the Haddington branch, stopping at Tranent and Longniddry on the way. For Musselburgh Races in July, trains only left the North Bridge Station 'at the Hours as circumstances will permit'. By October, the noise of trains crossing a bridge near the Palace of Holyrood House provoked complaints from the 'Office of Her Majesty's Woods & Forests'.

Within four days of the North British opening, the Edinburgh & Glasgow Railway appeared on the scene. For that company reaching central Edinburgh was no mean achievement. An Act of 4 July 1844 had given permission for a line conferring *'Public Advantage and Convenience'* to be extended *'from its present Termination near the Haymarket to the North Bridge…'*

But there were conditions. Crucially, the E&G was not allowed to erect any buildings at its terminus higher 'than

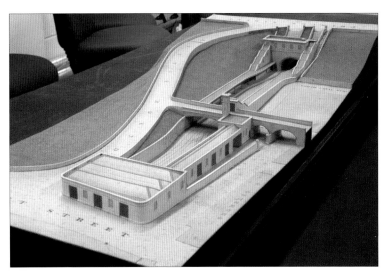

Above: A model of the projected Canal Street Station of the Edinburgh, Leith & Granton Railway, showing a land claim from Princes Street to Market Street, with the Scotland Street tunnel (top right). (Glasgow Museums Collections)

Left: The Bank of Scotland, sited on the Mound from 1806, was a demanding neighbour after part of its garden ground was taken up by the railway. (Thomas Begbie)

Thirty Feet above the Level of the Railway'. This restriction arose from the law of 'servitudes and ancient lights' that protected owners of property from obstructions being placed within their views. There was opposition from the Bank of Scotland, whose Head Office had been located on its prominent site above the Mound since 1806. A 'Station House', approved by the distinguished architect William Henry Playfair, was limited in both height ('five Feet below the level of the Carriageway on Princes Street') and length. Such structures as an 'Engine House, Manufactory or Workshop…calculated to create a Nuisance to adjoining Property' were forbidden. Only coke, a relatively smokeless fuel, was to be used for working locomotives through Princes Street Gardens and engines must not race there. A road built at an awkward slope of 1 in14 with arches beneath would give access to the yards at the E&G station. As arbitrators

This sketch shows a train on the Edinburgh & Glasgow Railway entering the tunnel bridge at the Little Mound with the newly erected Scott Monument (left). Canal Street Station with its steam winding engine and Scotland Street tunnel may also be seen. (A.J.S. Paterson)

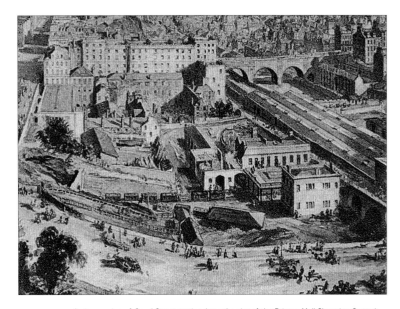

An impression of Canal Street station (now the site of the Princes Mall Shopping Centre), showing the station, winding house for a steam engine (right centre) and the Scotland Street tunnel with a train (left). The long train sheds of the first Waverley Station are seen on the right. (After C.Ebsworth)

John Miller would represent the Edinburgh & Glasgow, Thomas Grainger the Edinburgh, Leith & Newhaven interest, and Isambard Kingdom Brunel, the distinguished engineer of the Great Western Railway, would be asked to adjudicate if their opinions differed.

Under the 1844 Act, the Edinburgh, Leith & Granton Railway had acquired sweeping powers, including the taking of lands assigned to the Edinburgh, Leith & Newhaven in 1836. The E,L&G had so far failed to appear in Central Edinburgh but a model of its Canal Street proposals dating from 1849 shows its presumed site as stretching from

Princes Street on the north across the valley to Market Street on the south. For the loss of this prime area, it was hoping to receive £60,000 in compensation from the Edinburgh & Glasgow and the North British Railway companies.

On the E&G line, a 1,009yd tunnel immediately east of Haymarket had to be formed using gunpowder and brute force – tunnelling was not an exact science. Then the residents of Princes Street had to be placated with landscaping, plantings and high walls that would make the railway 'undiscoverable' from their drawing rooms. After that, contractors were faced with the Earthen Mound, the 'mud brig' between the Old Town and the New, a line of communication 'of great public accommodation and convenience'. Described nevertheless as 'this huge deformity of lumpish length', it consisted of excavated materials from the New Town, estimated at two million cartloads. It was a perplexing site with William Playfair's classical Royal Institution of 1826 (now the Royal Scottish Academy) on its north side, but the Mound had to be cut through with a tunnel of 124yds. Then came the former bed of the Nor Loch, drained in 1763 and planted with trees and shrubs as a pleasure garden in 1821. Inevitably, there were more protests. Finally, further east at the Little Mound, a three-arched bridge was inserted in order to meet the North British tracks end on. Its 'great centre arch' of 65ft was stone built and, being on piled ground, it settled 'about 4 inches'. The area of tracks to be placed on both sides of the Little Mound was firmly specified.

On 1 August 1846 the Edinburgh & Glasgow extension was opened to what was already appearing on maps as 'Waverley Bridge'. This location became in practice the site of a joint station. With E&G and NBR trains converging at this point, it was destined to become the foremost rail hub for

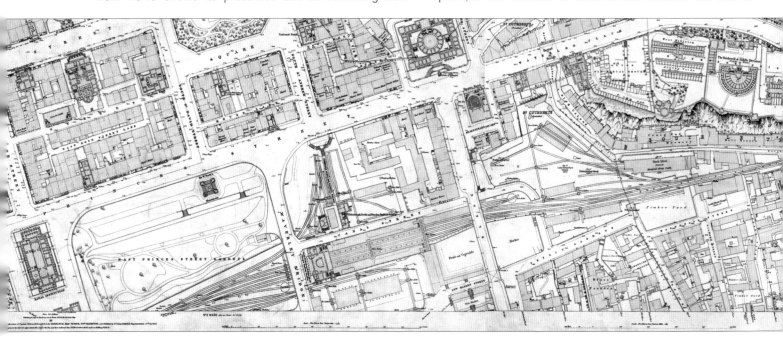

Part of the Town Plan of Edinburgh by the Ordnance Survey (1:1056) published in 1853, showing Waverley Station, Canal Street Station and the North British Railway's territory east of the old North Bridge. (National Library of Scotland)

passenger traffic in the capital, and in time just 'Waverley Station'. However, for many years the North British continued to refer to its own station as 'North Bridge'.

By 1846, the speculative bubble in railway shares had burst. As this was before limited liability protected shareholders, much money was lost. Enthusiasm for new lines therefore cooled. Yet within days of the opening of the NBR main line in 1846 that company had obtained Acts to build seven branch lines. However, these would prove only weak producers of revenue and incur additional costs of maintenance. (By 1848 Hudson, the Railway King, had been dealt a further blow by trade depression and forced into bankruptcy).

The Edinburgh, Leith & Granton Railway pressed on towards the city centre. After encountering adverse geology and the need to drill shafts in the sensitive New Town, plus problems with utilities, a long steep tunnel – 1,052yd at 1 in 27 – was excavated. This was the crucial portion from Scotland Street to Canal Street (so close to Princes Street) and the fact that it was gas-lit caused further objections from New Town residents with dwellings above it. The Scotland Street Tunnel was masonry lined and its trains used cable haulage powered by a stationary steam-winding engine at Canal Street. Special trucks with brakemen on board slowed the descent down to Scotland Street itself. (The intention had been to use steam locomotives but initially none was ordered. However, horses could not cope with heavy vehicles on steep gradients and lighter carriages had to be bought leading to even more expense). Recalling the tunnel, Robert Louis Stevenson wrote:-

'the site of the trains shooting out of its dark maw with the two guards on the brake, the thought of its length and the many ponderous edifices and open thoroughfares above, were certainly of paramount impressiveness to a young mind'.

However, the cavern was initially 'an irresistible attraction' for the more adventurous citizens.

Edinburgh, Leith & Granton station at Canal Street was finally opened on 17 May 1847, thereby giving Central Edinburgh three stations within walking distance of each other. Canal Street was crammed into a small site of about 100 square yards with room for just two short platforms, some goods sidings and wagon turntables. It was the last to arrive, squeezed out by the Edinburgh & Glasgow. The parties now faced each other across Canal Street – the E,L&G station, a two storey building, influenced by Playfair and in neo-classical style, befitted the city's claim to be 'the Athens of the North'. It was accessed by a steep ramp from Waverley Bridge and by two sets of wooden steps from Princes Street. (There had been some steps from the 1800s enabling citizens to negotiate the steep bank from Princes Street to Canal Street and the Little Mound). A tight curve led westwards from the E,L&G station onto the E&G lines. By November 1849 that company also served the market and manufacturing town of Bathgate.

To integrate Canal Street rail services with steamers to

The North British Railway's extensive goods yard with its small signal box (right) below Calton Hill with a locomotive in the foreground – a view from the late 1850s. (Thomas Begbie)

Kirkcaldy and Aberdeen, there were through coaches to Leith via the Edinburgh, Leith & Granton Railway that linked with twenty-five trains out and back on the Edinburgh & Glasgow. Passenger numbers were encouraging at first but the novelty of descending the Scotland Street tunnel with sparks flying from the brake wagons soon wore off. E,L&G business was also badly managed. By 1 April 1849, the Edinburgh & Northern Railway, a company with a thriving ferry and rail network across the Forth into Fife, had absorbed it. Here was a trunk route to the north to satisfy entrepreneurial aims and that April it emerged under another more ambitious name – the Edinburgh, Perth & Dundee Railway. It would soon boast the first roll on-roll off rail ferry in the world.

By the autumn of 1846, the NBR had faced severe setbacks – floods wreaked havoc with its poorly constructed line to Berwick and further strained its weak finances. Bridges collapsed and embankments were washed away. The engineering of the line by John Miller and the NBR's engineer James Bell was not in question – the deficiencies arose from the inferior work of contractors. The company had also recently embarked on a line to Hawick, on the back of the branch line Acts obtained that year. The tracks first used part of the old Edinburgh & Dalkeith from Niddrie to Newtongrange, the NBR converting this to standard gauge. The new route then followed awkward valleys and terrain to reach its 888ft summit at Falahill. From there, the meandering Gala Water led to the Tweed valley. With viaducts, numerous bridges and two tunnels to construct, the route was expensive to build. Nevertheless, Hawick was reached on 1 November 1849. The station at Melrose, giving tourists access to Scott's beloved abbey, was the most elaborate on the line.

The North British line to the Borders was not just about scenery and tourism as this was only seasonal – it was also a coal railway. Before the line opened, coal had to be brought by horse and cart to such mill towns as Galashiels, and the nearest supply was 24 miles distant. The mills, making cloth and woollen goods, were largely dependent on waterpower from unreliable and sometimes tempestuous rivers. Bringing coal from the Lothians by rail enabled investment in steam power that was followed by expansion in production and employment in the Border towns.

North British business was on the increase in Edinburgh and more land was urgently required at its terminus. However, the venerable structures of Trinity College Church and the Orphan Hospital, dating from 1460, stood in the way. Both buildings had royal associations but since the Reformation had been owned by the Town Council. Their demolition in 1848 was decried by Lord Cockburn who wrote:-

'The last and finest Gothic fragment in Edinburgh…will disappear for the accommodation of a railway …An outrage by sordid traders virtually consented to by a tasteless city and sanctioned by an insensible Parliament…'

Although the Town Council received compensation of £20,000 from the NBR for the re-erection of the church, it was never rebuilt. Eventually in the 1870s, some of the carefully numbered pieces of masonry were used at Chalmers Court, off the Royal Mile, where Trinity Apse may be seen today.

Meanwhile, the North British and Edinburgh & Glasgow trains were meeting at the modest two platform through station between Waverley Bridge and North Bridge. It was a timber structure on an iron frame, probably similar to the train shed now at the Bo'ness & Kinneil Railway. The station had a longitudinal slated roof with numerous smoke vents. There were five sets of rails with many little turnplates allowing small 4-wheeled vehicles to be reversed. The booking office for the E&G was on Waverley Bridge and the NBR equivalent was near North Bridge while their cramped goods stations lay beside Market Street and Waterloo Place.

Although the North British had secured Parliamentary authority for its main line at its first attempt, lack of finance was for long an issue for the company. It coloured NBR attitudes, leading to decisions being deferred. The directors had a reputation for being parsimonious with a preference for low cost solutions. The situation at Waverley was to demonstrate this repeatedly – the deficiencies were well known but for decades minimal improvements took place.

Of crucial importance to the North British was the lucrative Royal Mail contract that had to be honoured at all costs. In 1837, the year in which Queen Victoria came to the throne, an Act was passed for 'the Conveyance of the Mails by Railway'. Mail contracts were to prove vital sources of income for emerging railway companies, including the NBR at this stage.

The Edinburgh & Glasgow station in neo-classical style at Waverley Bridge in the 1860s; a masonry bridge of several arches goes through the Little Mound and the premises of the Edinburgh, Perth & Dundee Railway at Canal Street are on the left. (Thomas Begbie)

In September 1849, it was announced that Queen Victoria would travel south over the NBR line after holidaying at Balmoral. There is speculation that a 'Royal Engine' was painted in a tartan livery but certainly a stand for 600 guests was erected at North Bridge. This was the first of many royal visits to the Edinburgh terminus. Later, for the Queen's use, 'a very temporary station' would be put up on the south side of the line near Holyrood – in 1851 this structure was decorated to resemble an Arabian tent. Facilities at the North Bridge Station do not seem to have been considered suitable for a royal personage.

When the North British opened to Berwick, there was no rail connection southwards. By July 1847 the Newcastle & Berwick Railway was already at the south bank of the Tweed where passengers boarded an omnibus to cross the river. At this date, the train carrying the Royal Mail was the fastest service going south from Edinburgh. It left at 4.26am and took seventeen hours to reach London. For passengers, the journey was tedious but after the Royal Border Bridge was opened by Queen Victoria on 29 August 1850, 'international' traffic began to grow.

By the 1850s, the two 'expresses' to London on weekdays took fully 12 hours for the journey of 402 miles (via Lincoln and Spalding). Scots travelled by the thousand to the Great Exhibition of 1851. Tourism was growing and Black's 'Economical Tourist of Scotland' with its 'accurate travelling map & itinerary' had already appeared in several editions. Although holidays for most people were limited, 'cheap excursions' were promoted from Edinburgh and extra trains were run on 'Fast Days', the holidays before Communion Sundays. It had even become worthwhile for Thomas Cook to set up an office beside the E&G station in Edinburgh.

Goods traffic was already considerable in the 1850s. Top

An impression of the North British Railway's 'Crampton' locomotive in tartan livery as used on a Royal Train. (C.Hamilton Ellis/Harper Collins)

of the list was coal from the Lothians, minerals being the NBR's biggest source of revenue, and its wagon fleet had grown to 1,600 vehicles. North Bridge Station and yards were busy places with fish trains and consignments of fruit and vegetables in season. Every Monday a cattle train left Edinburgh for Newcastle. Wednesday markets could see 800 cattle and up to 2,000 sheep, being driven through the streets to pens at the yards. There were also trains conveying newspapers and parcels.

On occasion the relationship between the North British and the Edinburgh & Glasgow companies was fraught. In November 1853 there was a Court of Session case that disclosed that the E&G had been doing deals with the Caledonian Railway Company, the NBR's fiercest competitor. Amalgamation between the E&G and the CR was clearly in the air as they had joint arrangements for ticketing with

Below: The Royal Border Bridge at Berwick-on-Tweed, opened by Queen Victoria in 1850 was a key element in promoting the East Coast route. (John Peter)

Viewed from Princes Street Gardens, the widened tunnel bridge at the Little Mound and sidings for a variety of rolling stock are seen. The main station buildings are far left. (Thomas Begbie)

shared purses. A legal decision then prohibited the CR from using the station 'at or near the North Bridge' as its terminus in Edinburgh. It was stated exclusively to be the joint property of the E&G and the NBR.

In 1854 a Physic Garden on the south side of the stations and the slum of Low Calton to the north were cleared to make way for further railway facilities; yet these additions were soon not enough. (The Physic Garden had come into being in 1676 to give training in herbal pharmacy to medical students; it is now commemorated in a plaque adjacent to Platform 11 at Waverley Station). With the growth in rail traffic on the E&G, access to its goods warehouse and sidings was greatly improved by the partial reconstruction of the masonry Waverley Bridge. An additional south arch was first considered in 1856 and two years later construction was in progress. Images by Thomas Begbie, one of

Edinburgh's pioneering photographers, record the work.

In 1855 a new chairman of the North British board had been appointed. This was Richard Hodgson, MP for Berwick and a Border squire. Energetic and totally committed to the railway, remarkable improvements in performance and revenue were initially achieved during his regime, with the assistance of a capable general manager and locomotive superintendent. Hodgson viewed the Caledonian Railway as the arch enemy and his policy was to neutralise and, if possible, outflank that company. During his rule – described as resolute and remorseless but unscrupulous – the NBR mileage increased dramatically from a 58-mile main line with some branches to a system having 781 miles of track and equipment worth over £22 million.

By May 1860, with traffic continuing to grow inexorably from branches and extensions, the NBR's situation in Edinburgh was becoming well nigh impossible to manage. To try to improve matters at North Bridge, the company promoted its 'North British Railway (Stations) Bill'. Sir William Johnston, a former Lord Provost, appearing before a Select Committee of the House of Commons, stated that 'the delays at the station are very frequent and are caused entirely by want of room' – it always being worse in summer. 'We have been as long in getting from the tunnel (at Calton) to the platform as in travelling six miles'. Passengers found 'when we do get to the station, we land upon a narrow platform covered with luggage and sometimes merchandise from a train that has just

Left: A plaque in Waverley Station recalls the Physic Garden that among other properties was taken over by the North British Railway in its expansion. (Ann Glen)

given place to ours …Trains for the west are missed…'

Consequently, negotiations with the Town Council to obtain the site of their 'Green Market' for wholesale fruit and vegetables began. The old North Bridge had eleven arches of variable size, three being large. While one big arch was used by the NBR, the other two were occupied by market stances. In evidence, John Miller, the civil engineer, said that the NBR's station was 'dangerously small' and that he had been 'very much alarmed, more so than at any other station in the kingdom' in coming into it. Meantime, the number of people using the Green Market was 'a mere trifle' compared with the volume of passengers in the NBR station. Furthermore, there was only limited accommodation for the livestock trade. He feared what would happen when new lines in Fife were opened – the congestion at Waverley could only become much worse.

In giving evidence to the Select Committee, Miller was followed by Charles Jopp, one of his trainees and an engineer to the NBR since 1850. Jopp had prepared plans for an enlarged station. He recalled that some adjustments had been made to the premises in 1846, 1851 and 1856 but these were never enough. Jopp described the existing arrangements with five lines of rails in a train shed 140yds long and barely 40yds wide, the centre line having to be kept clear for goods trains to go through. Under the booking office and Waverley Bridge, there was a notorious platform just 45yds in length and only 3ft wide in places. Elsewhere limited space was encroached upon by rows of iron pillars and long E&G trains had to be divided to utilise short platforms. Furthermore, the sharp rise up from the east through the Calton Tunnel only 'increased the inconvenience of the station'.

Thomas Rowbotham, the NBR's General Manager, was quite candid – the platforms were 'really dangerous' with as many as eighty-six regular trains passing through each day plus numerous excursion trains 'of a very heavy character' in summer. In August 1859, the NBR's passenger numbers at North Bridge had averaged over 4,000 per day. If only the Green Market on the south side could be taken over, the bulk of the goods traffic could be transferred there, the company would get rid of shunting to the tunnel – and the Green Market site was the only piece of level ground available for expansion.

The NBR had other deficiencies. Its preoccupation with extending its network had led to insufficient attention being given to basic matters – its engine fleet was sadly deficient and locomotive superintendents came and went. Then in 1862 the newly opened line from Hawick to Carlisle became part of the famed 'Waverley Route' and the pressure on the terminus in Edinburgh increased even more.

Arguments continued over the station's unsatisfactory state but in January 1863 the NBR was reported to be 'contemplating change'. A line direct to Leith and Granton via Abbeyhill had been proposed. Although half a mile longer

The north portal of Scotland Street tunnel where a goods yard was latterly in use until the 1960s. (Author's Collection)

than via the Scotland Street tunnel, this new route would be 'more expeditious', saving time and being safer for passengers. Accordingly, the tunnel with its rope haulage would 'no longer be required, will be entirely disused and shut up as soon as the new line is formed'.

If parliamentary sanction had been obtained, the NBR initially proposed to place a large station on the vacated site, latterly the property of the Edinburgh, Perth & Dundee Railway. It was now 'partly waste' between Princes Street and Canal Street (where today's Princes Shopping Mall stands). A new station would be exclusively for passenger use and an opportunity to create much better NBR facilities in Edinburgh. W.H. Barlow, the eminent engineer to the Midland Railway, who was then occupied with the design of St Pancras Station, had been consulted. He proposed a radical solution – a completely new station on Princes Street Gardens' north side and the conversion of old Canal Street to a coal depot. Both were unthinkable for the NBR in terms of finance, and for the city authorities in terms of amenity, and were ruled out.

Meanwhile in the 1860s, the description 'the station at Waverley Bridge' had come into use. In September 1863 when the Inverness & Perth Junction Railway opened and sent trains on 8½ hour journeys from Inverness to Edinburgh, it advertised two stops – first at the Edinburgh & Glasgow station at Haymarket and five minutes later at Waverley Bridge Station, the joint facility with the North British. Only experienced passengers knew where best to disembark.

In 1864 the rivalry between the North British and the Caledonian was reaching new heights with the companies vying for the lucrative traffic between Edinburgh and Glasgow. Whenever an additional train was timetabled by the Caley, the NBR immediately introduced a similar one. Shortly, there were no fewer than 54 trains between the cities on weekdays, many of them empty; some expresses took only 65 minutes. After months of skirmishing and money wasted, sense prevailed and timetable compromises were reached.

For some years the North British directorate had been preoccupied with Bills for amalgamation with the Edinburgh, Perth & Dundee Railway. By an Act of 1862, the NBR absorbed that company and, in an agreement with the North Eastern Railway (NER), obtained access via Hexham to Newcastle – this in return for giving the NER the right to haul Anglo-Scottish through trains between Berwick and Edinburgh with NER engines and crews. (Such running power agreements were not uncommon and were thought beneficial in preventing the monopolies that Victorians deplored). In 1865 the NBR learned that the North Eastern would use its running powers to Edinburgh. However, only in February 1869 did this actually happen after adjustments had been made to platforms, water cranes and other facilities at Waverley to suit North Eastern locomotives. Though not without disagreements, it was an arrangement that lasted for over fifty years.

The impasse over the unsatisfactory conditions at Waverley Station took time to be resolved. The Edinburgh, Perth & Dundee's old Canal Street station, being close to both the NBR station and Princes Street, became a useful bargaining chip. By 1865 a Bill to authorise agreements about its use between the Town Council of Edinburgh and the North British Railway was tabled.

That year was momentous as the numerous early Scottish railway companies were amalgamating and five distinct entities emerged – the North British, the Caledonian, the Glasgow & South Western, the Highland and the Great North of Scotland. Crucially, the NBR absorbed the prosperous Edinburgh & Glasgow and the extensive Edinburgh, Perth & Dundee Railway while the Caledonian took over the Scottish Central.

For the NBR, there was reorganisation to face and Waverley Station, now being a joint property, was at last to have some improvements. To share responsibilities, James Bell, the company's engineer-in-chief, would oversee former North British interests while James Deas, chief engineer for the Edinburgh & Glasgow, would do likewise for his company. Both men had trained and worked with John Miller. Decisions had to be made about uniforms for staff and comparisons between the two companies showed how mean the NBR had been – some grades only getting coats and others no garments at all. Thankfully, the more generous practices of the E&G were followed by the NBR for its new 'corporate identity'. Waverley Station would become a North British stronghold for fifty-eight years.

The new goods shed (foreground) is an indication of the importance of revenue from freight traffic for the North British Railway in the 1860s. (Thomas Begbie)

A Station fit for a Capital

Times were changing and in 1866 after no less than seven years of discussion, the Town Council of Edinburgh agreed to a land transfer, or 'excambion' in Scots law, whereby the North British Railway won the coveted Green Market site. It was a deal in which no money passed – a satisfactory outcome for the NBR directors. In parting with the old Canal Street location to the Town Council, they believed that they had got a bargain – the prize being an extensive area destined to be a big goods yard and sheds. Whether this was a wise decision in the longer term for Waverley's passenger business is questionable.

A new fruit and vegetable market had to be created at NBR expense where the old premises of Canal Street station had stood. This was formed 28ft below the level of Princes Street with a solid embankment of sufficient strength to bear 'any superincumbent buildings which may be placed upon it'. A strong retaining wall was necessary against which the NBR constructed booths and stores for the stallholders.

Some Edinburgh citizens took exception to a market being close to Princes Street but others thought it preferable to the 'bare bank, scraggy grass and wooden stairs' of the 'intolerable and disgraceful' old station. So in 1869 an open-air market for traders was opened. Stone steps were installed – the famous Waverley Steps – to give access from Princes Street to the market and to the station. The Scotland Street tunnel was kept and continued into the station by 'sufficient arches'.

Soon a barrier to stop traffic on Canal Street made plain NBR rights under the 'Edinburgh Station & Market Act 1865'. Ever keen to make money, the NBR leased out the station cabstand on the north side for £450 a year, 'subject to any alteration the Directors may make on the station'. With the number of trains on the increase, a reliable water supply was another issue and authority was given to lay an enlarged pipe to bring water from the Union Canal to supply steam locomotives at Waverley Station.

By 1865, the NBR was in Fife, in Glasgow and had reached Carlisle but such expansion came at a heavy price. Investment in more lines had meant cutting expenditure ruthlessly on the maintenance of existing routes and on rolling stock.

Even so, by March 1866, the NBR directors were considering an entire reconstruction at Waverley. Being in doubt as to the shape this should take, they held an

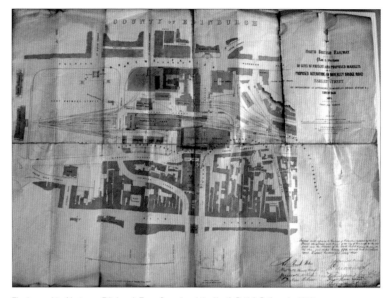

The 'excambion' between Edinburgh Town Council and the North British Railway in 1865 – pink shows the area of the 'Green Market' and brown the former site of Canal Street Station. (NAS, George Heriot's Trust)

architectural competition with a top prize of £350; this attracted several entries, all being anonymous. However, the competition was won by Charles Jopp, an NBR civil engineer. Monuments to Jopp's work are the tall 19-span Leaderfoot viaduct over the Tweed and the 15-span Shankend viaduct on the Waverley Route. It was hoped that any plan for 'Waverley Station, Hotel and Market' would be refined to be as 'perfect as possible'. Jopp's scheme was estimated to cost

The replacement 'Green Market' with its stances on the former site of Canal Street Station in the early 1870s. (Thomas Begbie)

This 1860s view from Edinburgh Castle shows the single tunnel through the Mound with the National Galleries of Scotland (foreground centre) and the market stances installed on the former site of Canal Street Station, adjacent to Waverley Bridge. (J L Stevenson Collection)

between £80,000 and £90,000 but money for such a major investment could not be raised – by the autumn of 1866 the NBR was in the throes of a funding crisis. In May of that year the failure of the Overend Gurney bank in London had precipitated a financial collapse; the economy went into recession with railway stocks badly affected.

In fact, the finances of the NBR had been in disarray for many years and the practice had grown of massaging the accounts to conceal deficiencies, giving an impression of well doing to maintain shareholder confidence. To offer a modest return (thereby supporting the share price on the Stock Markets), interest on stock was being paid out of capital. When a new company secretary 'blew the whistle', the scandal broke. The damage to the NBR's reputation was incalculable and plans for Waverley, its principal station, were

The old North Bridge (left) with North British lines squeezed through the arches while an access to platforms is also seen (centre). (Thomas Begbie)

put on hold. Hodgson and his fellow directors were forced to resign. A new board was appointed that was committed to a policy of rigorous austerity. A Committee of Investigation found that 'misrepresentation, deception and the deliberate falsification of the accounts', had been going on for years. Some argued that the directors should be imprisoned; this financial debacle was to haunt the company.

However, for the railway, a more efficient linkage with the port of Leith, compared with Scotland Street tunnel, was a positive move. This was at last obtained when just east of Waverley Station a curving line was completed from Abbeyhill on the East Coast route down to Trinity and the Forth. This branch was opened for goods traffic on 2 March 1868 and shortly saw its first passenger trains. The old tunnel could then be shut but was used for storing wagons while the station at Scotland Street itself became a coal and goods depot.

In the summer of 1868, the new NBR directors received the jolt of competition. This was in consequence of the Caledonian Railway opening its Mid-Calder line in July that year – meaning a fresh surge in the number of trains between Edinburgh and Glasgow. The NBR again altered its timetables in response. There was also another factor to concentrate minds – the North Eastern Railway had begun running its own engines on trains direct from York to Edinburgh and its directors were thoroughly unimpressed by the arrangements at Waverley Station. Accordingly, they made representations to the NBR board 'anent the limited accommodation provided at the Waverley terminus'. The NBR directors were reported as 'willing and anxious' to respond but were deterred 'by the present financial position of the company from spending any large sum of money on the station'.

To make matters worse, the Caledonian Railway then announced its intention to erect a new Edinburgh terminus at Lothian Road that would compete directly for Glasgow traffic. So, with the NBR directors having overlooked passenger comfort and safety at Waverley for years, all of a sudden alterations there became 'imperatively necessary'. When shareholders were informed that £50,000 would at last be spent on improvements, some expressed regret that double that sum was not being expended on an entirely new station.

So with 'the limited and unsatisfactory accommodation at the Waverley Bridge Station' having been a longstanding cause of complaint and adverse press comment, further thought had to be given to its deficiencies by the near insolvent NBR. By November 1869, James Bell, the company's Chief Engineer, had made yet another 'general plan' for a new station. This was ambitious and would not be fully realised until 1873. Preparing for increases in traffic, the station site would now stretch from the west side of Waverley Bridge through the North Bridge to Leith Wynd, an old alleyway running north-south between the Old and New Towns. A key element was the replacement of the masonry Waverley Bridge at the Little Mound with an iron beam structure. Indeed, the Little Mound itself would be entirely removed. In January 1869, the engineering profession had received a severe shock by the collapse of the first Tay Bridge in a winter storm. That structure had been a strategic part of the NBR system. Bell had therefore to take no chances with a bridge over lines at a busy station within a city centre.

The main access to the station would be a broad carriageway descending from a new Waverley Bridge and aligned towards the south of old Canal Street. Constructed

A view of the old North Bridge in the 1860s showing the congested circumstances in which the North British Railway ran its passenger and freight business. (Thomas Begbie)

on a ramp, this would allow passengers in cabs to be driven alongside the railway carriages 'without the disagreeable necessity of descending a flight of stairs'. The two-storey booking office, refreshment facilities (the Ordnance Survey records the Rainbow Tavern) and waiting rooms for First and Second Class passengers faced a paved area.

The station was now 'one sided' like Newcastle-upon-Tyne with the main platform of 'immense length' on the north flank having four lines of rails for through traffic. East of the booking office, short platforms or 'docks' were designed to

Left: The demolition of the Waverley Bridge at the Little Mound took place about 1872. The station building and stairs descending from Princes Street to the old Canal Street Station are also in view. (Thomas Begbie)

Below: The old North Bridge from the west showing (left) the glazed cast iron roof in transverse ridges, the footbridge access to the South Suburban platforms, and the roof of an old goods shed. (Blyth & Blyth)

hold Leith and local passenger trains, while west of the new Waverley Bridge, there were similar facilities for Bathgate and Queensferry trains. Altogether, the platforms could permit twelve trains to board or discharge passengers at the same time 'without more bustle and confusion than is caused by a single train'.

Being mindful of the 'ancient lights and servitudes' restrictions, the plan was to cover the main platforms with a roof of cast iron and glass now permitted to a height of 40ft above the rails. This roof was devised west of the old North Bridge by the engineers Blyth & Cunningham, under the supervision of James Bell. Benjamin Hall Blyth was a notable consulting engineer to many early Scottish railways. His practice, established in 1848, flourished on his expertise in giving evidence at Parliamentary enquiries on Railway Bills. In the 1850s, his brother Edward and George Miller Cunningham led the consultancy, and by 1869, Blyth's son – Benjamin Hall Blyth, Junior – was a partner. Experience in a major station project at Waverley was to stand the partnership in good stead.

Stretching 'in one great span' with ridges and furrows running north-south, the roof was similar in style to that at Victoria Station in London. To support it, strong but plain walls had to be built on either flank. On the south this had

rectangular pillars with masonry infill. On the north side, a wall bordered the now closed Canal Street. East of the North Bridge, there was no protective roof at all and passengers were soon protesting about this deficiency.

From these descriptions, a new configuration for Waverley Station emerges. The reconstruction was criticised for overlooking aesthetics, a fact of which *The Scotsman* complained,

'If the station buildings could be constructed on some uniform plan, both as to frontage, height and general features of architecture' how much better they would be.'

Exposed masonry walls, for example, should be accented with 'slightly ornamented arch work' in a classical style. Perhaps this nod to architecture may be seen in practice in the walls of the present station. At least platforms were cleared of the clutter of bothies, lamp rooms and the like, while old office accommodation became service facilities for clerks, porters, kitchen staff and left luggage. By March 1870, the work had been 'rapidly pushed forward but done piecemeal to provide for current traffic' – in other words, the reconstruction was being carried out when trains were running.

The significance of freight shows in the scale of the goods facilities installed on the south side. These absorbed

The new Waverley Bridge, a 'light construction of cast iron', replacing the tunnel bridge, was opened in 1873. The original station had been partially removed. (Author's Collection)

not only the Green Market but also the old Edinburgh & Glasgow goods station and were equivalent in area to the passenger station. The new goods shed had 'a large loading wharf', and a 4-storey warehouse with two lower levels was designed to fit between Market Street and Waverley Bridge. With the entrance from Market Street now closed off, there were 'lines of rails by which through goods trains and locomotives may pass outside the passenger station'. Special facilities were made for the important 'cattle traffic department' on the south side, and for the mails from the General Post Office on the north.

James Bell's Waverley Bridge, 'a light iron structure' with stone abutments, took shape. Its suppliers were Hanna, Donald & Wilson of Paisley, iron founders and bridge specialists since 1851. For some decades, cast iron, despite its imperfections, was the foremost construction material. The bridge formed 'an improved access to the New Waverley Passenger Station', and a link between the Old and New Towns as it met the new Cockburn Street on the south. Once a temporary timber bridge was in place, stone foundations for the new structure were 'sunk to a considerable depth'. The main girders rested on three rows of iron pillars, giving ample space beneath 'for general station purposes'; the spans varied in width 'to suit the exigencies of the railway which here spreads out like a fan'. As the new bridge was wider than the old, the central portico of the original neo-classical booking office was removed, only two wings being kept for parcels offices.

In February 1873, a ceremony took place whereby the Lord Provost and Town Council formally accepted the roadway and footpaths on the new Waverley Bridge from the North British Railway – but only after the Burgh Engineer had checked the measurements to ensure that these were the statutory width. Then the cabbies and drivers waiting with their horse-drawn vehicles, vans and carts rushed to be the first across. The bridge cost £20,000 but, courtesy of the railway, the citizens had obtained a better road 'without a farthing of expense'.

The NBR retained ownership of the bridge itself. However, it was unsatisfactory for passengers giving only a modicum of protection to the west facing platforms.

Questions were asked in a letter to *The Scotsman*:-

"Should Edinburgh's visitors not be made comfortable when arriving or leaving the city? Pity the poor passenger …chances are he has to get wet before taking his seat in a carriage, causing discomfort to men and risk of illness to women and children".

Railway stations were invariably 'cold draughty places' with platforms 'wet and sloppy' after rain or snow. Nevertheless, the placing of verandas over the west platforms was contentious. Surely roof canopies could not be worse than the lines of empty carriages and coal trucks held in sidings west of Waverley Bridge? In fact, the NBR

Parts of the cast iron and masonry at today's station may have been reclaimed from earlier structures. (Ann Glen)

should be persuaded to cover *all* the space over its tracks between the Mound and Calton Tunnel constructing brick arches throughout with grass on top.

At the renewed Waverley Station, traffic kept growing and some passengers received special attention. For example, Queen Victoria and her extended family's journeys through Waverley were noted in the press. Railway companies vied with one another to produce suitable vehicles – indeed, whole trains – for royal use but Victoria insisted on travelling in six-wheeled coaches, bogies being unacceptable. Along its route, the Royal Train was given priority by means of 'Special Working Arrangements', causing disruption to other services and to station business. A pilot locomotive ran ahead and 'company servants' were positioned at intervals along the line side. On the other hand, a Royal Train was not always used – the Prince of Wales was observed travelling on 'the Aberdeen ordinary train' in November 1869, doubtless a relief to those who organised royal transits. Foreign royalties, the titled, ambassadors, distinguished politicians and celebrities of the day were

A 'romanticised' postcard view from Edinburgh Castle shows the Waverley Station of 1873. (Bank of Scotland/Lloyds Bank Archives)

regularly mentioned as arriving at Waverley or departing from the station.

Each year, the busiest time was the Edinburgh Trades' Holiday, the first fortnight of July, when platforms swarmed with passengers – such a throughput called for as many as 1,000 trains per day in and out of Waverley. The General Assemblies of the Church of Scotland, the Free Church and other religious gatherings saw throngs of clergy and representatives of congregations at the station. The Fast Days before the twice-yearly communions in April and October, when many people took a holiday and travelled to visit friends or family, continued to put pressure on facilities.

Excursions to Edinburgh were very popular even if some arrived and departed from Waverley at unsocial hours. The tourist trade was expanding with ten hotels on Princes Street alone while many more had opened in streets near the station. Edinburgh's fame rested on 'its natural beauty, its unique site and the many objects of interest around it', all of which attracted visitors, especially in the summer months. When the old Post Office building on Princes Street was converted to a hotel (it also took the name 'Waverley'), its large hall could seat 800. Excursion parties arriving by the first trains from the south at 3.29am could then be conveniently 'breakfasted' there – the station's modest refreshment rooms could not cope with such hungry hordes.

An innovation that the North British could rightly claim was the introduction of a sleeping carriage, the first in Britain. This six-wheeled vehicle from an English builder was a speculative purchase by the NBR. It had two sleeping compartments, trimmed in crimson velvet with silver plated fittings in 'sombre grandeur', plus a washbasin and water closet – such toilet facilities were rarities on railway vehicles at the time. There was also a passenger compartment for servants and provision for luggage. To give a quiet journey in the heavily built vehicle, its fixing to the frames involved India rubber while thick carpeting covered a patent underlay. The sleeping carriage first set off from Glasgow Queen Street via Edinburgh Waverley for London Kings Cross on 2 April 1873, patrons paying a 10s supplement. However, neither the press nor the public were enthused and it eventually became East Coast stock. Four years later, the NBR would be one of the first railways in Britain to fit continuous brakes to passenger carriages. This was a major investment in safety and the Westinghouse air brake's thumping sound would come to characterise Waverley Station and its locomotives for many decades.

When carriages had no corridors or gangways (vestibule connections) at either end, tickets could not be checked *en route*. For expresses coming from the East Coast, trains stopped briefly at Portobello where there was a ticket platform that allowed staff to access compartments for this

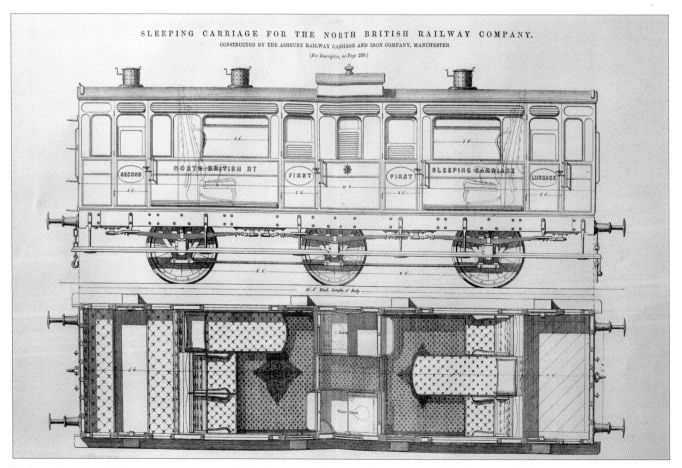

The first sleeping carriage in Britain was introduced by the North British Railway on through services to Kings Cross in April 1873. (Engineering, 1873)

purpose. This performance was reckoned to add seven minutes to journey times. There was a similar arrangement for trains from the west at Haymarket. Once vestibuled stock was introduced, ticket platforms were abandoned and tickets were inspected on board trains.

If there was money to be made, the North British would put on extra services and this it did in January 1876 with trains departing from Edinburgh at 11pm to give 'country residents the opportunity to witness the pantomime'. In May a Masonic Ceremonial in the capital also called for extra

trains as Masons received special attention and were 'conveyed to Edinburgh and back at a Single Journey Fare'. 'Lodge Waverley Edinburgh 597' was established in February 1877, and while not restricted to railwaymen, they dominated it for many years. In summer the NBR advertised excursions to places throughout its growing network. Old 'picnic coaches', fitted with U-shaped benches, were brought into service and thought 'convivial' for parties though 'singularly uncomfortable'. Workman's trains were much worse and could have as many as twenty-two vehicles, all

Left: After 1876 the Waverley Route to Carlisle was accessed by the Midland Railway. A NBR engine on an express with Midland & North British Joint Stock carriages nears Edinburgh. (Author's Collection).

Below: The NBR faced 'make-do-and-mend' policies; here a rebuild of an Edinburgh & Glasgow 2-2-2 locomotive is seen beside Princes Street Gardens in the 1890s. (J.L. Stevenson Collection)

The Waverley Market, a cast iron structure with roof gardens, was completed in 1877 at a time when horse-drawn trams plied in Princes Street. (Author's Collection)

four wheelers, recalled as 'hen coops on wheels'.

At the other end of the spectrum, in August 1876 a 'Pullman Car Holiday Party' left Waverley in their 'palace carriage'. Pullman cars were an American innovation and in 1870 the enterprising George Pullman had come to Britain. He arranged to supply the aspiring Midland Railway with Pullman cars in kit form in order to introduce luxury travel on its services. Down the years, trains of Pullman coaches came to epitomise *grand luxe* on railways and Waverley got its share of such traffic.

The year 1876 saw the fulfilment of a North British ambition. At the commencement of the company in 1845, the Bill contained a reference to powers for an extension from Hawick to Carlisle. By 1859 the NBR board was considering how to restrain the rival Caledonian Railway from tapping into territory northeast of Carlisle. The Border Union project seemed to be the answer, although it was criticised by many shareholders and commentators who saw little point in it. Such a line with long viaducts, steep gradients and sharp curves would be costly to construct, to operate and to maintain. Furthermore, south of Hawick, it ran through sparsely populated upland country where revenue possibilities were very limited. But this was a 'political' railway, a means of check mating the Caledonian. For the NBR directors, that was an overwhelming advantage and in 1862 the lines at last reached Carlisle and the NBR quartered itself at Canal Street in that town.

The shareholders' adverse views about the Border Union Railway were to soften when the wealthy Midland Railway completed its Settle & Carlisle route from St Pancras to Carlisle in 1876. The Midland was ambitions and this was its opportunity to come north across the border with a main line operation. As it also hated the London & North Western Railway, the Caledonian's West Coast partner, the Midland and the North British could comfortably join forces. Thus 'The Waverley Route' could come to the fore and on 1 May that year a through service between London St Pancras and Edinburgh Waverley commenced. Forthwith, the North British began advertising 'eight day Cheap Special Excursions from Edinburgh Waverley Station To St Pancras Station, London, by the Waverley and New Midland Route'. Pullman cars and sleeping carriages soon appeared on it.

By 1878, there were two London expresses out and back from Edinburgh over the Waverley Route each weekday but there were complaints about North British time keeping and criticism of its comfortless 'shaking' carriages on local trains. The line may have wound its way through the 'Scott country' famed in song and legend, but it was a slow route. The Midland had come late to main line action and its trains were often slower than those of other companies but it compensated

for this with greater passenger comfort and amenities. By 1872 it was annoying competitors by carrying third class passengers on *all* its trains. It soon got rid of second class and its third class stock became *upholstered* – leading to the charge that the Midland 'pampered the working class'. By 1874-5 the company was building bogie coaches, turned out in crimson lake, for its 'Scotch traffic'. These 'Joint Stock' carriages were said to 'run like a dream' and gave a much smoother passage over the Waverley Route, but the NBR had to provide the engines from Carlisle north.

In 1875 the North British had appointed a new Locomotive Superintendent, a dour and determined Scot who became a legend. This was Dugald Drummond who successfully designed strong 4-4-0 engines for the expresses on the Borders route. These were given names of places on or near that railway and locomotives named '*Abbotsford*', Sir Walter Scott's home near Melrose, and '*Waverley*' soon appeared. The Midland Railway was quick to publicise the line as 'romantic and scenic', making it even more popular as a tourist destination.

Meantime, Waverley Market had been transformed from market stalls in the open to the site of a large cast iron building with a gallery. In 1877 its partially glazed roof was adorned with flowerbeds to make an elegant promenade in harmony with Princes Street Gardens. The market premises evolved into much more than a space for selling wholesale fruit and vegetables, indeed they became a hub for large public gatherings – social, political and religious meetings, exhibitions and displays (from menageries to motorcars) and an annual carnival – all advantageously close to Waverley Station. Crowds flocked off the trains to the events with a pedestrian access from the Waverley Steps for the energetic.

From the 1870s enamel signs began to appear on station walls and fences. These soon augmented the paper billboard advertisements of earlier years – enamel was not only colourful but also durable. Being 'impervious to the effects of weather, resistant to vandalism, and easily wiped clean',

such signs had a strong appeal to railway companies. The NBR and its railway rivals had no qualms about having fine masonry walls covered with such advertisements. The eye-catching designs also brightened the smoke-stained, drab interiors of stations such as Waverley. Today, the places where these signs and billboards were once fixed remain as filled holes.

The signs were made by a complex method involving sheet iron, metal oxides and glass. Birmingham firms pioneered their production but the Falkirk Iron Company was active in Scotland. Part of an advertising revolution, the signs took many products from relative obscurity to being household names and some had memorable jingles such as the famous products of McNiven & Cameron of Edinburgh:-

'They come as a Boon and a Blessing to Men,

The Pickwick, the Owl and the Waverley Pen'.

The company also advertised, *'The Flying Scotchman Pen'* (an early reference to that famous train) and *'The Scotch Express Pen',* to appeal to railway passengers.

Notwithstanding the Temperance Movement, Waverley Station showed advertisements for alcohol, such as McEwan's Famous Ales, Sandeman's Port, and Bell's Perth Whisky. The North British had already divided its advertising business into three sections – east, central and north. The displays earned rent for the railway company and the signs are now much sought after as 'collectables'.

Waverley's concourse soon had vending machines. Introduced in the 1880s, busy places such as railway stations with large 'footfalls' were ideal sites for them. The first 'penny in the slot' machines dispensed Cadbury's or Nestlé chocolate bars. There were also stalls on the concourse offering confectionery, fruit and tobacco. By 1857, John Menzies had many Scottish railway bookstalls, mainly selling newspapers, but not at Waverley on account of the 'exorbitant rentals' charged by the North British. However, in time, Menzies came to dominate at that station too. A penny was a useful coin to have around Waverley Station – it paid the 'basket boys' in official uniforms who

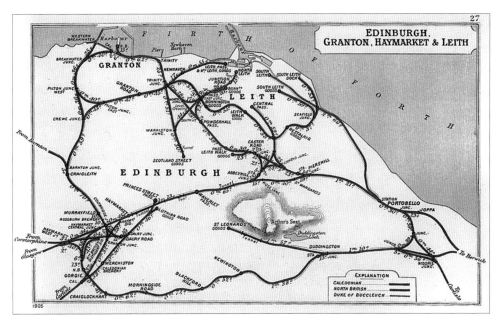

A map of railways around Edinburgh in the 1900s reveals the rivalry between the Caledonian and the North British Railway companies for supremacy. (Railway Clearing House)

Opposite page inset: From the 1870s enamel signs brought about an advertising revolution in Britain. (Author's Collection)

patrolled platforms and threw rolled up newspapers to passengers through carriage windows, it could purchase snacks for journeys, and it also gave access to station toilets.

In the autumn of 1884 the Edinburgh Suburban and Southside Junction Railway opened; it officially became part of the North British Railway the following year. In a letter to the Board of Trade, the NBR directors saw the new lines as

The east side of Waverley Station in the 1880s with Drummond designed locomotives and the signal box now positioned on a gantry. (Author's collection)

reducing congestion at Waverley – a means of ridding the main route between Haymarket West and Portobello of all through goods trains. They added cautiously, 'it will be many years until suburban passenger traffic be at all considerable'. However, when the passenger services began on a half-hour timetable they were well patronised by Edinburgh commuters.

That year the horse-drawn trams that had been operating in Central Edinburgh since 1871 were supplemented with cable-hauled trams – wire rope cables in channels between the tracks were powered by a stationary steam engine at a depot in Henderson Row. The trams had gripper devices to attach them to a continuous cable when they had to move, similar to the system in San Francisco. Would tramcars ever come to rival the railway? That may have made the North British directorate apprehensive.

The 'South Sub', as it was known, formed a 14-mile circular route south of Arthur's Seat and Salisbury Crags serving both leafy suburbs and areas of industry. Its stations were Gorgie East, Craiglockhart, Morningside, Blackford Hill, Newington and Duddingston; in addition, Portobello, Piershill, Abbeyhill and Haymarket were also on it. A regular service ran through Waverley where an island platform was made for the trains on the south side – the inner circle running east via Portobello and the outer circle west via Haymarket. (Nowadays Platforms 8 and 9 continue to be known to some citizens as the 'suburban platforms'). Easy access to these was made by having a staircase off Waverley Bridge – and special tickets were issued to office staff in the city to encourage them to 'go home for lunch'.

Nevertheless, Major Marindin, the Board of Trade Inspector, had misgivings about the arrangements on the 'South Sub'. While giving permission for facilities – the new island platform and two additional through passenger lines – he noted that re-signalling with the interlocking of points and signals had at last been done at Waverley. Over the years, the station had seen accidents, mishaps and near misses, most arising from complex shunting moves. The signalling deficiencies had been an ongoing concern. The Major then commented,

"The fact is that the whole place is cramped and inconvenient …nothing less than an entire reconstruction of the station, and probably the removal of the goods yard altogether, would make a thoroughly satisfactory job. As to what has been done, it is a great improvement on the old state of affairs".

By the latter 1880s, the Scotland Street tunnel had found a new use. It was tenanted by the Scottish Mushroom Company that used a line of rails to bring in wagonloads of horse manure (of which the city was glad to be rid) and to take out the produce for the local market. The cultivation demonstrated 'sustainability' until 1929 when production ceased owing to fungal disease.

The NBR had concerns about fire hazards at Waverley Station. Large quantities of esparto grass were handled in the goods yard for the paper, printing and publishing trades for which Edinburgh was famed. The dried grass was inflammable but in August 1885 fire from another source made headlines, 'Gas Explosion at Waverley Station'. The NBR manufactured oil gas to light its through carriages using an installation from 'Pintsch's Patent Lighting Company'; this was housed in a small corrugated iron building. Josef Pintsch was a German inventor whose discovery in the 1860s was taken up by railway companies. The brighter light from the gas soon replaced oil lamps in vehicles but it was highly flammable making rail accidents much worse. At Waverley, the gas was prepared and then stored in an iron tank that fed pipes to reservoirs underneath carriages – these were filled just before the trains left. A sudden 'flare up' partly destroyed the iron building with workmen and firemen injured.

Waverley Station regularly saw the coming and going of troops as Edinburgh was and is a garrison town. After the Crimean War (1853-6), a Volunteer Force of part-time soldiers, organised in regiments, was created. In 1860, a Royal Review in Holyrood Park called for a major effort by the North British and the Edinburgh & Glasgow Railways. On 25 August 1881 there was another Royal Review, this time bringing 40,000 volunteers from all over Britain to Edinburgh. Special trains arrived from every quarter of the country and Waverley Station was stretched to the limit. By afternoon, skies that had been dull and overcast were deluging the city with rain. Spectators and volunteers were soaked to the skin and uniforms ruined in this notorious 'Wet Review'. Several succumbed on account of the drenching.

Sporting and celebratory occasions also made the railway busy. Edinburgh's football clubs began in the 1870s with the establishment of the Heart of Midlothian and Hibernian teams. The former drew its support mainly from industrial Gorgie, the latter from the Old Town and from Irish immigrants around the port of Leith. Both adopted association football rules and as their reputation grew, they

The Caledonian Railway's famous 4-2-2 locomotive No.123 (now preserved) whose performances in the Railway Races of 1888 became legendary. (A.E.Glen)

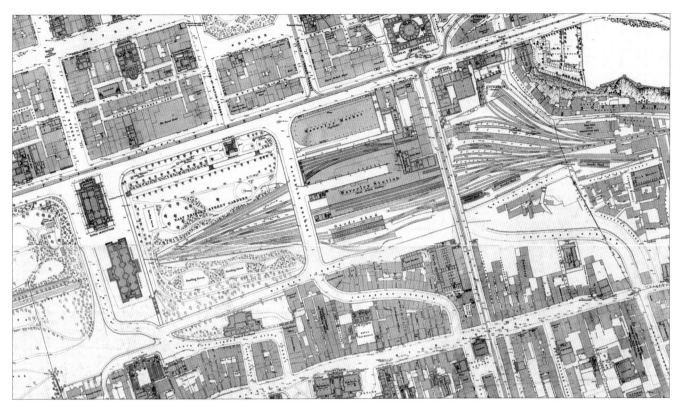

This Ordnance Survey Town Plan of 1881 shows the layout of Waverley Station after the reconstruction was completed in 1873. Only the portion west of the North Bridge was roofed over. (National Library of Scotland)

attracted crowds to their matches. Spectator sports were a welcome release from the confines of workshops and factories and by the end of the 1880s thousands of fans travelled by special trains to games 'home and away'. Then there was rugby football – the first international between Scotland and England was played in Edinburgh in 1871 and a Scottish Union was shortly set up. High points of Sunday School excursions were sports for youngsters and in 1885, William Paton, the Station Master, was reported to have 'despatched' 5,000 children in a day from Waverley on such local trips – Polton being a favourite destination.

There was also 'sporting' competition on the railway. On the East Coast route, faster runs by more powerful locomotives had been reducing the accepted timings. From 1862, the 10am train from London King's Cross to Edinburgh Waverley was shown in timetables as the 'Special Scotch Express' taking about 10½ hours. There was intense rivalry between the East and West Coast companies for Anglo-Scottish business – the East Coast being served by the Great Northern and the North Eastern, and the West Coast, by the London & North Western and the Caledonian. In early August, when 'the glorious 12th' was the start of the shooting season, northbound cavalcades of passenger vehicles, horseboxes and luggage vans, brought lucrative traffic through Waverley Station.

In November 1887 for the first time, third-class passengers were permitted to travel on the 'Special Scotch Express' from Kings Cross, a fact that the West Coast companies resented. But they thought they had an answer. In secrecy at midsummer the following year, a special train left

Euston at 10am and took just under nine hours to reach Edinburgh via the West Coast and Carstairs. The race to Edinburgh of August 1888 had begun. The final leg was behind the renowned Caledonian single wheeler No.123, now displayed in the Riverside Museum in Glasgow. The East Coast companies retaliated and set about cutting their times from Kings Cross to Waverley by an hour. Soon, the schedules for both were 9 hours with luncheon stops being taken at York and Crewe; shortly 8-hour runs were being made. Through media participation – journalists were on board the racing trains – the contests caught the public imagination. At that date, Edinburgh was the finishing line for the East and West Coast routes; the average speeds on the last lap to the city were over 57mph. It was good publicity, well timed to woo the sporting fraternity coming north. Crowds watched the trains, whetting an enthusiasm for railways among the public, but the honours overall were remarkably even. Before the winter, a new accord was reached whereby the East Coast timing became 8¼ hours and the West Coast 8½ hours, and these were maintained in the timetables for several years.

Meanwhile, the Caledonian Railway by an Act of 1884 had been developing a bold scheme for the Glasgow Central Railway that would be largely underground in the city's built up area. It had tackled such a project between Greenock and Gourock on the Firth of Clyde and now had confidence that it could carry out a similar one in Edinburgh. The idea of 'cut

The opening of the Forth Bridge in March 1890 placed further strains on Waverley Station and the tracks leading to it. (Peter Stubbs Collection)

and cover' tunnelling through Princes Street and its famous Gardens horrified citizens and alarmed the North British directors. A CR station was proposed close to Register House from where a tunnel would be driven under Calton Hill and thence down to Leith. By 1889 the threat was at its height and, owing to unsatisfactory services by the NBR, there was considerable support for the Caley's audacious project. (The CR even had an office in the General Booking Hall at Waverley where passengers could buy tickets for CR trains running from its own Edinburgh station at Lothian Road to Perth, Dundee and Aberdeen via Stirling).

The inadequacies of Waverley Station were well known – *'that huge sprawling callosity of the Princes Street valley…'* Passengers complained about having to run down 'dangerous stairs' – the Waverley Steps – or take a roundabout incline followed by a lengthy walk to the ticket office. The neglect of convenience and comfort by a mean-minded company was obvious. In summer, trains approaching the station could be held up at every signal and be very late. There was chaos and confusion:-

'Bewildered crowds of tourists sway up and down amongst equally bewildered porters on the narrow village platforms reserved for these most important expresses…while higher officials stand lost in subtle thought'. E. Foxwell and T.C. Farrer in *Express Trains: English and Foreign (1889)*

Waverley was rated the 'worst arranged and dirtiest station in the United Kingdom'.

Worse was to come. In March 1890 the Forth Bridge, praised as 'the unparalleled triumph of engineering', opened and the North British provided a special train from Haymarket to convey the Prince of Wales (later King Edward VII) and dignitaries to the ceremony. The strains placed on the minimal lines in and around Waverley Station soon became intolerable both to the travelling public and to the NBR's railway partners. Problems had been foreseen in the press a year earlier,

'The imminent completion of the Forth Bridge will throw all the north traffic of the North British Company on to the section between Waverley Station and Corstorphine that is already sufficiently crowded … if we may judge from the frequent delays that occur now …'. The Scotsman, 29 November 1889.

It was forecast that the *raison d'etre* for the great bridge, a direct and fast route to the north from Edinburgh, would be nullified by delays at or near the station. The NBR directors appear to have given little thought to the situation, taking up a 'wait and see' position. There was public cynicism – would the long-standing deficiencies at Waverley and its approaches ever be properly tackled? As an observer wrote,

'The new Waverley Station plans have achieved immortality, even if they never get further than being made on paper'. The Scotsman, 8 November 1890.

In April 1890 the NBR's Glenfarg Railway had opened from Mawcarse to Bridge of Earn – a crucial portion of line allowing the company to avoid using running powers over Caledonian tracks via Stirling to access Perth. Although the double track Glenfarg route was only ten miles long it had a steep gradient – going south there were over five miles at or close to 1 in 75. Construction was difficult calling for deep rock cuttings, substantial embankments, numerous culverts, twenty-two bridges and two tunnels. The route proved a brute to operate and the NBR had to double-head many of its trains over it. As for Waverley, the Glenfarg route simply inundated the station with new NBR services to and from Perth.

Protests soon came from the NBR's East Coast partners with angry telegrams being exchanged. First from the North

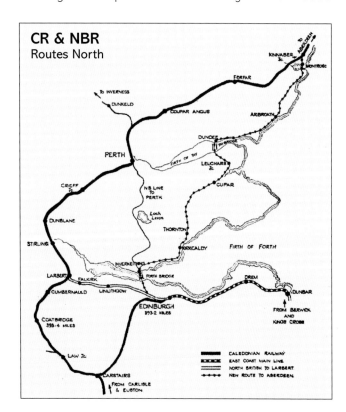

The Caledonian and North British routes to Aberdeen were followed in the Railway Races of 1895. (Ian Allan Publishing)

Eastern on 2 June 1890, 'Understand up Scotch express has had a late start this morning of one hour …Will you wire me the cause of this?' Next day, there was worse when the General Manager of the Great Northern Railway asked, 'What are you about? You are ruining the character of the East Coast. Let me hear what steps you are taking – reply at once. Oakley, Kings Cross'. Henry Oakley was the doyen of railway administrators and was knighted in 1891.

By 6 June, the Great Northern and North Eastern were both asking, 'What improvement may we expect in the working of the Scotch trains in the next few days? The present position is very serious'. There were implications much further a-field than the East Coast route whenever connecting services were held up or missed.

The North British tried to fight back, 'Ask them to run *their* down trains on time …the 8.38 due in Waverley did not arrive till 9.6. The East Coast newspaper train has just arrived an hour late'.

From the Midland Railway at St Pancras, there also came complaints. The North British apologised to its long time partner, 'Very much regret the delays but we are doing the best we can in the circumstances. It will take a few days to get the new arrangements into working order'. This was wishful thinking. There would be prolonged negotiations, an Act of Parliament and a great deal of investment before Waverley Station and its approach lines would be fit for purpose. The NBR understood where the problems lay – 'The great block to traffic is the inability to get trains in and out

of the station on the single pair of rails between Haymarket and Waverley and between Abbeyhill & Waverley'. And the company knew what the remedy should be, the quadrupling of tracks from Haymarket and Portobello into the station – 'the duplication of the lines will afford immense relief to the working of traffic. More sidings, not fewer are required'.

The public joined in the fray. A letter to the NBR's General Manager had offered a solution:-

'In view of the extraordinary block at the Waverley Station today, caused by the opening of the Forth Bridge through traffic & the absolute necessity for increased station accommodation, would it not be well for the company to acquire at once the Waverley Market & construct on it & on your present ground a Station suitable to the requirement of the City & your line?'

This would give scope for 'a magnificent station fronting directly on Princes Street and on the North Bridge', an echo of the Barlow proposal of 1862. The writer got an abrupt 'yours truly' reply.

Circumstances forced the North British to seek a different solution. On 5 July agreement was reached with Edinburgh City Council to rebuild Waverley Station more or less on its existing site and to improve track access to it. This meant diverting streets and acquiring additional land. An Act of Parliament of 5 August 1891 gave the NBR powers to reconstruct the station. Not without controversy and not without a struggle was the third incarnation of Waverley Station about to begin.

This 1880s view of Waverley's facilities east of the old North Bridge shows extensive carriage sidings (left) and a new goods shed on the 'green market' site (right). (Author's Collection)

Another New Waverley

The North British Railway was proud to announce its intentions for a 'New Waverley Station'. This was not an idle boast as the reconstruction would be radical. The removal of strips of land from Princes Street Gardens was again contentious, as was the additional tunnelling through the Mound – not surprisingly, both provoked civic outcry.

Restrictions remained on the building height within the valley. However, these 'servitudes and ancient lights', which the neighbouring Bank of Scotland sought to enforce, were now relaxed to 42 feet above the rail – still making the station as unobtrusive as possible. This was directly contrary to what railway companies had in mind – they envisaged imposing stations of architectural merit with soaring roofs, generous space for circulation and ample amenities for passengers, which would be powerful statements of their aspirations and worth. Waverley's new roof of glass, steel girders and iron gutters would fill a valley but have only a low profile. There would be no spectacular façade or grand entrance. Beneath the structure and within agreed limits, permission was given for refreshment rooms and other station accommodation. As for Waverley Market, the NBR were only to use any available land there 'for the storage of rolling stock and carriages and for no other purpose'.

The proposals for the 'New Waverley Station' were brought forward in difficult times for the Scottish railway companies. There was a strike in December 1890 lasting until the end of January 1891, the main issue being the long hours of drivers and firemen. An eight-hour working day was desired. With 8,500 men out, the strike's timing through the busy holiday period at New Year was calculated to cause major disruption and damage to revenue. The NBR was the last company to see its employees go back to work – possibly a comment on its industrial relations. Yet attitudes to working conditions and welfare were changing for the better, and Waverley Station had its own ambulance team.

To make any improvement to traffic flows at the station, ground had to be taken from both the East and West Princes Street Gardens. By May 1891 the land required, just 30ft (10m) in width overall, had been marked off with stakes and poles on both sides of the railway. There were protests as

A postcard view of the Waverley Station of the 1890s, a development restrained by the Bank of Scotland (right) and city interests. Note the tunnels under the Mound. (Author's Collection)

neither the Town Council nor the public had been given an opportunity of assessing any potential reinstatement; indeed, it was feared that the NBR directors were closing the door to negotiation. The company had offered to cover all portions of Princes Street Gardens given up to the railway with a roof on which parterres of flowers would be grown but the public was not impressed. According to the Town Council and many citizens, the existing gardens were 'priceless' – and if the NBR directors realised their worth, less would be heard about 'encroachments'. Although the biggest area required was on the north side of the line, including some Crown land, a little had also to be taken on the Castle side – from the War Office and the Bank of Scotland. The latter sought compensation both for its land and for the impairment of the view from its Head Office.

Of the 289 trains running west in a day from Waverley, 31 were goods trains (to which objection was taken) but there were also 68 light engines going to Haymarket for turning. A disturbing proposal had appeared – namely that a 70ft turntable should be installed in the gardens. This 'gratuitous outrage' was severely criticized as it would be the largest encroachment on the park and a potential scene of smoke, coal banks, water tanks and noise. Servicing locomotives there would be 'an unjustifiable nuisance' to

residents and park users. The NBR excused the idea as a suggestion from the 'English companies', the Midland and North Eastern Railways. Facing stern opposition, the turntable proposal was dropped.

However, there was considerable public support for sacrificing some garden land to ensure the safe operation of the railway – this must have precedence over amenity. The 'land take' of two acres (less than a hectare) was settled by arbitration in October 1892, the NBR paying £26,500, though the Town Council had at one stage asked for £150,000. There was a proposal to screen the railway with 'hanging gardens' to hide its 'naked ugliness' but, with practicality in mind, masonry walls topped by railings were built and trees planted.

Another stumbling block was the old North Bridge. This had constrained the NBR from its beginnings and £125 was paid each year for the privilege of squeezing lines through two of the eleven arches. The main up platform at its east end was just a ledge under the bridge. By April 1891 the

Right: Form work takes shape for the new North Bridge while North British structures (right) on the east side are removed. (Blyth & Blyth)

Below right: When demolition of the old North Bridge began, trains continued to run. A view to the South Suburban platforms with the goods yard on the left. (Blyth & Blyth)

Below: Land ownership at Waverley West, showing the northward claim of the Bank of Scotland in green. (Bank of Scotland/Lloyds Bank Archives)

Initial work on the north tunnel through the Mound shows a cast iron section in place. (NAS/BRB(Residuary)Ltd)

Engineer's Office could report that agreement had been reached with the Town Council whereby the NBR would contribute £30,000 – one-third of the cost – of a new North Bridge. Blyth & Westland, the same consulting engineers appointed to mastermind the new station, designed the imposing three-arch cast iron and steel structure on massive masonry piers. The Blyth practice had long been distinguished in railway engineering and by 1893 the partners were Cunningham, Blyth & Westland, although Cunningham shortly retired. James Bell, Junior, who had succeeded his father as the NBR's chief civil engineer, arranged the track work, platforms and signalling for the new Waverley Station, while James S. Pirie 'project managed' the entire works on behalf of the company.

At the west end, Waverley Bridge became a vexed issue. Having only seen its completion in 1873, the NBR directors were seriously discomfited when the consulting engineers announced that it would have to go. 'The removal of a bridge less than twenty years old?' They protested but the consultants stood firm – only its replacement by a larger structure would permit the desired arrangement of lines at Waverley Station itself.

Additional tunnels at Haymarket, the Mound and Calton Hill had to be cut. By March 1892 the Land Valuator was warning tenants to vacate their houses and shops at Haymarket. Again volcanic rock stood in the way, and blasting, not only of the tunnel but also of ventilation shafts, took place at night when trains were not running. Residents naturally protested and looked for compensation but the NBR was warned – 'no saying how many may come forward if anything is to be got'. The new south tunnel, with fine ashlar portals, was lined with concentric brick rings and came into use on 21 July 1895. Haymarket Station was also a focus of reconstruction being 'rearranged' to take four tracks. On the west approaches, bridges over the Water of Leith, over roads and railway lines, had also to be widened. Subsequently, a new 8-road engine shed with servicing

facilities and a turntable was built at Murrayfield, west of Haymarket Station.

The works at the Mound were another construction challenge. In 1859 the National Gallery of Scotland, a Playfair classical design, had risen adjacent to the Royal Scottish Academy (formerly the Royal Institution). Two additional single line tunnels would now be cut below this new building. The Mound consisted of 'forced earth' and in September 1892, James Carswell, the NBR engineer responsible, suggested using the 'shield process' with compressed air for the excavation, and lining the tunnels with cast iron segments. With the agreement of Blyth & Westland, a tunnelling expert engaged on the Glasgow Subway was asked to supply a tender for 'workmanship only', the NBR providing 'all machinery, engines, boilers, castings, bricks, cement and other materials required'. The directors quickly gave approval as it would 'take quite five or six months before we can get the machinery on the ground and the work fairly started'. While 'every possible precaution' was taken to avoid damaging the National Gallery, 'some unsightly settlements made their appearance in the west frontage'. Consequently, a large portion of masonry, including the heavy cornice and parapet, had to be taken down and replaced.

By October 1892 widening the track formation in the East and West Gardens was a priority as it was 'absolutely necessary to provide Sidings on both sides of the lines for

The additional Mound tunnels were constructed by the NBR using the 'shield process' and compressed air. (NAS/BRB(Residuary)Ltd)

the reception of the ballast trains…Wagons have also to be filled with excavated material and cannot stand on the main line'. Soon there were protests about ballast trains going round the South Suburban at night and disturbing sleep; a Night Inspector was appointed to try to quieten their passage. Nevertheless, the Mound tunnels were in use by 24 June 1894.

Preparations for an extra Calton Tunnel saw the clearance of property at North Back of Canongate, east of North Bridge. Described as 'little better than slums and ripe for removal', this was estimated to displace some 2,000 people. Of concern were two breweries whose premises had wells supplying artesian water on which the brewers' ales depended. Construction faced other difficulties – such as driving piles

23ft long into soft ground. On the approach to the Calton Tunnel the line had to be carried obliquely over long girder bridges. Below track level, extensive underground stores entered from New Street were made; these are now a car park. The new tunnel was formally opened on 28 June 1896.

Attention now turned to the station itself. In April 1894 work commenced on an extension to the existing North Wall where a siding was to be retained 'for storing the Dining Car Train', introduced the previous year. Eventually, the North Wall going east was a composite affair; it first concealed a hotel basement, then came a curtain wall followed by a long steel girder to span tracks leading into a loading bay for the Royal Mail. The concluding portion was a new masonry wall along Calton Road.

A strategic element for safe movement across Waverley Station was a mezzanine footbridge. Its south span was begun on a Sunday in 1894 by P&W McLellan of Glasgow, the principal contractors for the steelwork, when timber trestles were erected over the down main line. When completed, ornamental ironwork hid its heavy girder structure. Several other footbridges were essential to allow the flow of

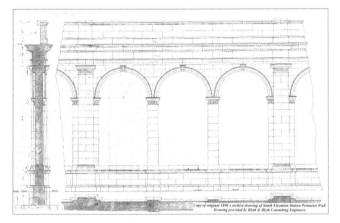

Left: The design for the Klondyke Wall on the station's south flank was neo-classical and used 'blind arcading'. (Blyth & Blyth)

Below: Construction proceeds on the new North Bridge with former North British offices on the right and the 1873 goods shed on the left. Adjacent to the south pier of the bridge, the new water tank is being built on top of the Klondyke Wall.
(RCAHMS/Sir William Arrol Collection)

North Eastern locomotives ran the East Coast services to and from Waverley Station. Here two NER 4-4-0 locomotives doublehead an express. (Author's Collection)

pedestrians and luggage through and across the station.

Tenders were soon invited from 'signal people' but this revealed some uncertainty about the overall plans for the new station:-

'It is quite time that the platforms and rails was decided upon …it will take a lot of time to get the necessary points and crossings made, besides arranging for the work generally…' John Carswell, engineer, North British Railway.

With eight bay platforms at the east end and seven at the west, the approach lines were to be interconnected by scissors crossings.

By July the consulting engineers were advising that provision must be made for a new station wall between the main and the suburban lines – the famous Klondyke Wall. The gold 'rush' by prospectors to the Klondike region of the Yukon in northwest Canada was at its height between 1896-99 – around the time that the wall was being built by G & R Cousin, builders from Alloa. Constructed as ashlar, dressed rectangles of cream sandstone concealed a core of rubble.

For Waverley employees, their 'Klondyke' may have been the spot where gold jewellery washed onto the line from basins in sleeping cars.

There had been Station Police at Waverley since the 1880s, usually dealing with theft. Pick pocketing had been rife from the 1860s when gentlemen's gold watches were targeted. Pilfering of ale, whisky and other items from goods vehicles in sidings tempted employees although culprits faced dismissal and imprisonment. Now amid the engineering decisions, there were more mundane matters to consider such as 'Accommodation for the Police Department'. Its staff now included a Superintendent, Inspector, Detectives and Policemen They were looking for larger rooms, a store and a lavatory, but the office location was crucial:-

'It is of the utmost importance that the offices are overlooking the platforms so that the superior officers …can see what is going on'.

It might be thought that the North British had enough on its plate with the rebuilding of its premier station and city terminus. Nevertheless, in 1894 it made known its intention to run the East Coast expresses between Edinburgh and Berwick-on-Tweed with its own locomotives. This was contrary to the old 1862 agreement with its East Coast partners. The Great Northern and North Eastern were appalled, considering it senseless to change engines at Berwick. So began one of the longest legal battles in the history of railways in Britain, elements of which went as far as the House of Lords. Out on the line, heavier trains were requiring regular double heading, or pilot assistance, and there was squabbling over timekeeping. The late running of down trains into Waverley badly dislocated Scottish internal connections, while up services to Kings Cross could rarely keep to time. Despite North British attempts to use its own

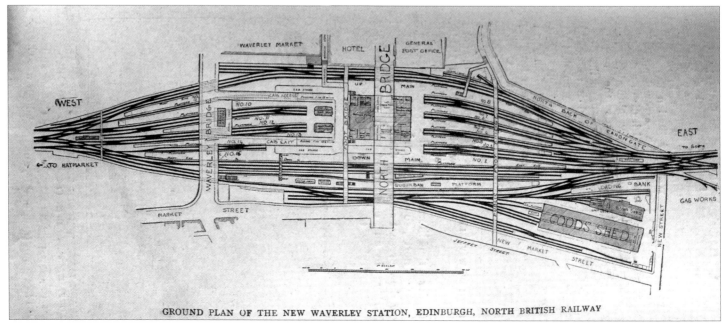

GROUND PLAN OF THE NEW WAVERLEY STATION, EDINBURGH, NORTH BRITISH RAILWAY

A plan of the new Waverley Station showing the 'double bottle neck' with through lines on either side of the 'island' and 'dock' platforms for local services at the ends. (Railway Magazine, 1900)

locomotives, by 1900 the North Eastern was firmly in control again and heading more trains on the East Coast main line in and out of Waverley than ever before.

Early in 1895 Waverley Bridge itself began to be taken down after a 'temporary wooden service footbridge' was erected. Meanwhile, the NBR had worries about the removal of the old North Bridge where men above the railway lines were 'working in twos and threes without any special provision being made for their protection'. The contractor, Arrol's Bridge & Roof Company of Glasgow, was reprimanded, the NBR stating, 'Our rule is that when our men are working in a Station Yard they are all in one Squad with a man to look after them...' Sir William Arrol's firm, famed for its construction of the Forth Bridge, was expected to follow NBR procedures.

Keeping the station itself in safe operation was difficult – there was annoyance from passengers when 'water was sent down' from Waverley Bridge on to platforms. The East Coast Traffic Superintendent asked for 'some protection' at his office to prevent stones and material falling from above 'when he was sitting right underneath…'

Arrols were again the contractors. As the bridge location was on the site of the old Nor Loch, foundations some 90ft deep had to be made. The erection of the steelwork was mostly done at night with a 'heavy travelling crane and sheer legs' running on the station tracks. A new Parcels Office had to be built. Of neo-classical design, its first floor was at bridge level with a yard at the rear, the storage floor below being linked to the platforms by hoists. Meanwhile, the wings of a station building were removed but a front was salvaged, thanks to Robert Morham, the City Superintendent of Works. It became an information office on the southwest corner of the new Waverley Bridge, where it still stands.

With an eye to economy, the decorative parapets of the old were re-used on the new Waverley Bridge. Ramps of steel girders (again built by Arrols) with cast iron balustrades, descended into the station, one leading in and one out; no space was wasted and premises for lamp trimming and other tasks were tucked underneath. Whereas these 'inclined cab approaches' with a gradient of 1in15 were not ideal, the area for cab stances was generous. Throughout the summer of 1895, work was pressed forward with 660 men and 120 horses plus carts in action.

The revamped Waverley West with its new signal box, imposing signal gantry and the new Waverley Bridge. (Author's Collection)

In October that year the engineers were confronting the problem of placing a mighty water tank on top of the Klondyke Wall by the south pier of the new North Bridge. The wall there was constructed with a 'double skin', forming a robust support with steel strengthening. Mackenzie Brothers, Edinburgh iron founders, supplied the 'cistern' of cast iron plates, with bracing and a timber cover, over a concrete floor. It was designed to hold 70,000 gallons to supply the entire station and thirsty locomotives on incoming trains, plus the small tank engines that acted as station pilots. These 'tankies' took empty stock in and out to carriage sidings at Craigentinny and were reckoned to be the hardest worked engines on the NBR system. (The Train Register in the East Signal Box showed that dealing with 'ECS', empty

North British trains racing along the widened tracks through Princes Street Gardens. (J.L. Stevenson Collection)

coaching stock, was a major operational task and continued so to the 1960s).

During dry periods, water shortages had been recurrent in Edinburgh but in 1871 a new Edinburgh & District Water Company took over provision in the city. By 1886 it had agreed to supply Waverley Station with water 'at a rate of 6d per 2,000 gallons with a reduction to 3d after the company has taken 18 million gallons', or paid £450. So taking water from the Union Canal declined. New sewers of greater capacity were placed under the station to give adequate drainage. Hydraulic hoists with steam pumping engines were installed by Armstrong, Mitchell & Company of Newcastle for luggage, parcels and the Post Office – all being heavy users of water.

Another 'Race to the North', this time to Aberdeen, was a distraction in the summer of 1895 and newspaper reporters were again out in force at Waverley:-

'The arrival of the two competing express trains from London to Aberdeen is still exciting keen interest…'

The record of 10 hours by the West Coast route was to remain unbroken even although the East Coast Route, thanks to the bridges over the Firths of Forth and Tay was 16½ miles shorter. When the racing train of seven coaches from Kings Cross with its North Eastern locomotives dashed into Waverley at 3.30am, it took only 4 minutes to change over to North British engines. Drivers relished working the expresses to Aberdeen. That city was being regularly reached in less than 3 hours from Edinburgh, but the Caledonian Railway, with a lighter train and even sharper working via Perth and Forfar, was arriving crucially 5 minutes earlier. The races were expensive for the companies concerned – a waste of competition – and questions were also asked about the safety of the racing trains. Soon new agreed timings for both East and West Coast services were in force and the races were consigned to history.

In February 1896 tenders were invited for the construction of 'the Roofs, Footbridges and Relative Works in connection with the New Waverley Station at Edinburgh'. By April, the old glass roofing was advertised for sale, *'Purchaser to be responsible for Taking Down and Removal of the Glass… Full Particulars From P&W MacLellan, Glasgow'.* The disposal of the wrought iron girders followed – 'could be used economically for Workshops or Buildings requiring the covering in of large areas…'

Such re-cycling helped to keep costs down which was welcomed by the NBR.

Left: A view across the west concourse at the rebuilt station with the north ramp on the right. (Glasgow City Archives)

Below: The extensive east roof of the new Waverley Station under construction with the supporting columns, lattice girders and glazing. (RCAHMS/Sir William Arrol Collection)

The roof, designed by Blyth & Westland, was rebuilt again in a transverse 'ridge and furrow' style using parallel lattice girders of steel. This time it was 375ft wide and 1,240ft long but short spans were essential – the girder depth was restricted to give as much headroom over the platforms as possible. The lattice girders were supplied by Hanna, Donald & Wilson of Paisley, a versatile company associated with the station since the 1870s. Tensioned steel rods gave wind strengthening and cast iron gutters rested on wooden blocks. McLellans, the structural engineers, were a prominent firm that had risen from humble beginnings in 1805 at a hardware shop in Glasgow's Trongate. By 1844 the McLellan brothers were manufacturing iron goods including nuts, bolts and rivets for Clyde shipbuilding. Within a few years they were making iron bridges, thus beginning their interest in structural engineering. In 1883 they won a contract for approaches to the Forth Bridge, thereby giving them their first experience of steel. By the 1890s McLellans was a public limited company with over 3,000 employees.

That year a tender for glazing the roof came from the Pennycook Patent Glazing & Engineering Company. Set up in Glasgow in 1878, it had pioneered the use of roof trusses and steel stanchions to create large glazed and waterproof roofs without putty. However, lead was used extensively. Major stations, such as Glasgow Central, Perth and Dundee (all for the Caledonian Railway), plus public buildings and factories at home and overseas, were among the Pennycook projects. The contract of 23 March 1896 was with McLellans for *'roofs of the main station with No.1 Galvd. bar & 5/16 rough rolled glass including overlaps and all cutting to the extent of 410,000 super feet (more or less) at the rate of 11¾, eleven pence three farthings per foot super, less 5% direct'*.

When glazing was completed by 1 May 1898 and after a period of maintenance, the glass was to be left 'clean and in good order'– a similar obligation bound McLellans. During roof construction, the latter gave assistance in hoisting materials with their cranes, 'wherever practicable'; however, they looked for an order for 'bolts and nuts' as part of the deal. Finally, teams from Maxon & Carfrae applied three coats of paint to the roof structures.

A corner of the new main building showing its blend of architectural styles and some revenue earning kiosks. (Glasgow City Archives)

The west concourse with its two large kiosks and the twin ramp access. (Glasgow City Archives)

The mighty roof was supported on tall cast iron columns with elegant Corinthian capitols, the castings being supplied by the Widnes Foundry, a Lancashire company established in 1861. The columns rested on deep foundations and also had a basic function – they concealed down pipes for drainage from the roof. By January 1898 'large girders for the extensive operations' were brought to the station in 'a heavy special train' from which they were lifted into position by cranes. A curious provision was a lattice footbridge in the roof structure from Calton Road across the width of the station to Jeffrey Street. It replaced a Right of Way, known as Leith Wynd, between the Old and New Towns that once went under the railway lines. When the NBR's new goods facilities were developed in the 1870s, this historic route had been lost. The Town Council now insisted on a replacement and – conveniently for the railway company – had it constructed at its own expense.

Meanwhile, west of Waverley Bridge objections from a nearby hotelier stopped an overall roof being installed in place of the low verandas above the platforms. So the west platforms continued to give Waverley the character of a rural station, which they do to this day.

The new North Bridge progressed and the foundation stone was laid at deck level with full Masonic honours on 26 March 1896. The structure was praised by the City Council both for carrying water mains and for allowing cable tramcars to run on a wide roadway. From the NBR's perspective the new bridge definitely simplified the operation of the railway, but this was not always apparent to passengers. A 'Daily Traveller' commented on 'the perfect chaos at Waverley' and the puzzle the station was to strangers when so many new platforms were being created. In 1902 platform information

The signal boxes at Waverley Station:
1. Waverley West 2. Waverley East 3. Waverley North Central 4. Waverley South Central on the Klondyke Wall. (J.L. Stevenson Collection)

A staff photograph at Waverley Station in 1905 with Station Superintendent W. Paton and his assistant (with top hats), the inspectors and foremen. (NAS/BRB(Residuary)Ltd)

boards (devised by NBR engineers Benn & Cronin and operated electrically from the signal cabins) were introduced in an effort to assist people. These showed the platform number at which trains from the south and east would arrive.

Waverley's new main building, now in the midst of an immense island platform, was also designed by Blyth & Westland, with some input from Herbert Raithby, their young architectural assistant. Cousins of Alloa were again the builders. In *fin de siècle* style, the station's new centre piece was three storeys high and built to impress. It had many functions – booking hall, refreshment rooms, waiting rooms, lavatories, (duplicated for first and third class), left luggage and offices, yet it ingeniously hid a central pier of the new North Bridge. The spacious booking hall was in fine sandstone with a mosaic floor showing the North British Railway's coat of arms at its corners. There were high windows and a stained glass dome with figures and garlands in *belle époque* style on the frieze below. All this was unusually exuberant for the NBR. A massive octagonal pavilion in dark wood, housing the ticket offices, took centre stage. There were heraldic flourishes on the stonework and a bronze statue of John Walker, the General Manager under whose auspices the new Waverley Station had been begun. Soon model locomotives of the new NBR Atlantic 'Auld Reekie' and of Stephenson's 'Rocket' were on show.

Many hundreds of men were now employed at Waverley. In charge was the Station Superintendent with a team of Inspectors, Foremen, Guards, Signalmen, Porters and Lamp Boys; over 300 worked at the passenger station alone. The Goods Station and Depot had almost as many employees. There was an army of clerks in the offices and on the top floor was the Telegraph Department with forty lady operators – their employment said to demonstrate the value of 'the emancipated woman'. Each day they sent out some 4,000 messages to help run the complex North British system; the public could also have messages sent – if they paid for them.

Beneath the station, capacious cellars concealed bothies, canteens, stores and boilers. Before the days of steam-heated trains, 'foot warmers' were available for passengers travelling in chilly carriages in winter. These devices were basically tin bottles containing soda acetate crystals that had to be prepared by immersing the container in boiling water. Surprisingly, the new rooms for guards and porters were placed very close to the station's wine cellars.

The increase to four lines at each exit, the so-called 'double bottle neck' effect, with many times that number of sidings and docks at platform ends, resulted in 'an enormous number of points and signals'. These were controlled from four signal boxes – two hung on walls in the station itself and two were close to the tunnel mouths at either end. The Board of Trade had approved a scheme for 228 points and 290 semaphore signals on gantries straddling the tracks. The east box reputedly had the longest continuous signal frame ever constructed – it had 260 levers; the west box

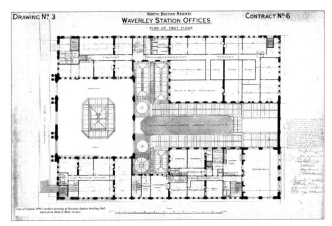

Top: The ground floor plan of the new main building at Waverley Station. (Blyth & Blyth)

had 205 levers. The signalling installations alone cost £24,000, a big expense at that date.

By 1899, the great reconstruction was nearing completion. The NBR was rightly proud of what had been achieved on the constrained and difficult site. The company had spent £1½ million and Waverley was now stated to be the largest railway station in the United Kingdom. It had a glass roof of 11½ acres in extent, 'its ridges like waves on a sea', while a further 6½ acres were left uncovered. Only London's Liverpool Street and New Street in Birmingham were near rivals. Electricity had replaced gas lighting. The goods station on the south flank, which now handled mainly perishables and newspaper traffic, was 5 acres in area with seven sidings, a large goods shed, warehouses and numerous cranes.

Combining a terminus with a through station was not easy. There were two main platforms 560yds long on either side of the central island that also accommodated local trains at 17 dock platforms. The two 'through' suburban platforms on the south side were long ones. Altogether the station's platform length was over 2½ miles; the platforms might be wider than hitherto, but some new surfaces were just wooden planks. Typically 630 trains were dealt with daily and Waverley was reckoned to cost £33,000 a year to run.

The booking hall with its eight-sided ticket office in dark wood, its florid ceiling and mosaic floor. (Paul Anderson/Irwell Press)

The North British Station Hotel

With the NBR debarred from having a majestic station in the Waverley valley, the company resolved to have an imposing hotel, a building that would soar above the East End of Princes Street to complement the new North Bridge and dominate all around it. In addition, it would have a dramatic view across the gardens to Edinburgh Castle, the Old Town and further a-field to coast and country. The NBR did own some hotels – nine modest hostelries (two being temperance ones), but this new hotel would be in an entirely different league.

A limited architectural competition was held in 1895 that attracted the foremost Scottish architects of the day. Rowand Anderson, J.J.Burnet, William Leiper and Dunn & Findlay had all created notable public buildings; both Rowand Anderson and Burnet would subsequently be knighted. The Edinburgh architect William Hamilton Beattie was selected for the commission as he had experience of hotels and in 1893 he had re-designed Charles Jenner's Department Store on Princes Street, a building in close proximity to Waverley Station.

A 'Hotel Committee' was set up to investigate the latest hotels in Europe and take forward the project for the 'Terminus Hotel' – a name that was soon changed to the 'North British Station Hotel'. A party of four, including the NBR's General Manager John Connacher, plus the architect, set off to tour Europe's capitals and great cities – Berlin, Vienna, Budapest, Amsterdam and Brussels were on the list. The Grand Hotel at Gare St Lazare in Paris was a hit with the NBR party. Five storeys tall and in the highest style, it was equipped with electric light and lifts. It had cost the equivalent of £320,000 but shops on the ground floor could produce useful rent. After seeing this *tour de force,* London's railway hotels failed to impress the NBR visitors.

There was an obvious site for the new hotel – where the NBR's old offices stood at the corner of North Bridge and Princes Street. These and adjoining premises were demolished to make way for the hotel. Thankfully, the proposed building did not incur the disapproval of the Bank of Scotland as there was no interference with sight lines from the Mound. The design was said to be 'a rendition of Renaissance architecture' but the Cockburn Association criticised the flamboyant mix as 'bad taste'. It protested about the very high clock tower proposed – a 'Big Ben' for the capital – and insisted on a height reduction to protect the view to Edinburgh Castle from Calton Hill.

Cousins of Alloa were chosen as builders. The site was on rock and when work began in January 1897, the first night's blasting broke windows in the adjacent General Post Office and severely shook buildings on Princes Street. Excavations as much as 20ft below the level of the railway had therefore to be cut by hand and took time. The hotel's south wall had then to be speedily constructed in order to avoid impeding the construction of the station roof.

The scheme suffered two sad reverses. The architect became fatally ill and was succeeded by his brother George Beattie and chief assistant Andrew Robb Scott. In March 1898, during a gale, there was a collapse of timber scaffolding on the south wall when there were three fatalities and serious injuries to a team of bricklayers.

The North British Station Hotel took four years to build and cost over £559,055. Constructed of dressed sandstone, its tall tower was surmounted by a crown 183ft from street level. The tower carried a large clock – a timepiece kept two minutes fast to help passengers catch their trains. The Hotel Committee had to do battle with the General Manager and Company Secretary to prevent the NBR setting up offices in part of the building. Such an outcome would 'seriously injure the hotel' and the committee eventually won the argument – there would be no shops on the ground floor or offices overlooking the station that might spoil its palatial qualities.

Every step was taken to make the building fireproof – using

Above left: A view to the new Waverley Station with the North British Station Hotel (left) and the garden roof of Waverley Market. (Author's Collection)
Above right: The Palm Court of the new hotel, decorated in 'the highest style' according to contemporary taste. (RCAHMS/Scottish Colorfoto Collection)

a steel frame and concrete for floors, arranged around a white-brick central court. There were coal cellars below, supplied by a chute from a wagon in the station. There were boilers for hot water and central heating but the public rooms had fireplaces. Steam heating was also piped to sleeping cars stabled in the station. Electricity powered eight elevators, fans for ventilation and the cold store; generators in the basement gave sufficient energy to light the station. The bedrooms had electric light but with typical NB economy only one light came on no matter how many switches were pressed. The hotel had an in-house laundry and a staff of over 100, 'men sleeping out' and 'women sleeping in' when 'inferior rooms' were found for their use.

In spite of the tensions between the Hotel Committee and the directors, ultimately, the interior was fitted out in opulent fashion with elaborate plasterwork, marble flooring, mahogany panelling and silk hangings in the public rooms. The Grand Staircase was designed for 'dignity and accessibility' with an entresol for 'proper perambulation' – being seen was to be part of the experience at this hotel.

Although solidly Victorian, the hotel was innovative – from its Palm Court lit by a cupola and its Coffee Lounge to its American Bar in the basement. Discussions about furnishing these and stocking the cellars (with the sampling of liquors on offer) occupied many meetings of the Hotel Committee. With 391 bedrooms, the new hotel was more commodious than any other in Scotland – indeed, of Britain's station hotels at that date only St Pancras was larger. Bathrooms were shared unless a suite was hired and there were several of these, being 'arrangements for gentlemen desirous to reside in the city'.

On 15 October 1902 the North British Station Hotel

Top right: A North Eastern locomotive with an express at the Down Main platform. Note the advertisements on the Klondyke Wall. (Author's Collection)

Above: The west platforms at Waverley with a NBR Atlantic (4-4-2) locomotive No.876 Waverley, and a 4-4-0 on trains waiting to leave. (T.Harden Collection)

Below: While fishwives with their creels sit by the main building, hansom cabs wait for fares. (Glasgow City Archives)

opened. An advertisement on the front page of *The Scotsman* proclaimed:-

'This HOTEL in DIRECT COMMUNICATION with the WAVERLEY STATION will be OPEN for the RECEPTION of GUESTS ON and AFTER TO-DAY THURSDAY 18th instant. F.T. BURCHER, Hotel Manager'

The 'Direct Communication' at the station was by means of corridors and lifts, one for guests and one for staff. Advertising was also carried in newspapers in London, New York and Paris. A lavish dinner for 280 invited guests was held in celebration of the hotel's opening but the NBR was to discover that running such an establishment successfully was a costly business. While the summer months could be expected to be profitable, there were worries about filling the hotel the rest of the year. Would balls and banquets in the function suites ever supply enough business? Grillrooms and tearooms were soon highlighted as additional attractions.

Even so the NBR could not shake off its rival, for at the West End of Princes Street, the Caledonian Railway was building its own sumptuous hotel in red sandstone beside its new Princes Street Station. This competitor, at a strategic crossroads in the city, opened in 1903.

In 1902 the platforms at Waverley for local trains were 'gated'. Barriers were already in use on the London Underground and at some major railway stations. Once Waverley's huge glass roof made it 'enclosed', it was reported that 'loafers' took advantage of its shelter in wet weather. The long platforms were 'an excellent promenade for young folks', with romance resulting. The 'non-passenger frequenters of the station' confused staff and fraudulent travel was a particular problem on the South Suburban route. So unless a valid ticket for travel was produced, a platform ticket costing a penny was now necessary. However, there was free access to the main 'up' and 'down' platforms where people met or saw off passengers on the long distance trains.

Hard as work was, station staff found time for recreation – the clerks had a cricket team, the shunters played the cleaners at football and in 1902 the goods clerks organised a ping-pong tournament (table tennis, then a novelty) and won. The ambulance team held annual suppers and 'smoking concerts'.

For the rebuilt Waverley Station there was no official opening but on 12 May 1903 the new King Edward VII, accompanied by Queen Alexandra, arrived there on the Royal Train for a state visit to Edinburgh. *The Scotsman* reported:-

'Waverley does not seem to give much scope for decorative effect … but by means of a wealth of shrubbery, pot plants, flags and crimson draping, the southern or main down platform had been beautified and brightened almost beyond recognition…spiral garlands of evergreens were wound round the iron pillars, and at the foot of each was a mass of tall shrubs, relieved by collections of pot plants in bloom'.

On the platform, the King was presented with the keys of the city by the Lord Provost. From a publicity perspective, the ceremony was very positive for the NBR – at last the company had a station in Edinburgh of which it could be

Above: The State Visit to Edinburgh by King Edward VII in 1903 gave the North British Railway a royal occasion at the new Waverley Station. (Illustrated London News)

Upper right: A view into Waverley Station from the east shows the structure of the roof with its supporting columns; note the narrow platform with a wooden surface. (Glasgow City Archives)

Lower right: A NBR Atlantic No.877 Liddesdale powers through Princes Street Gardens in pre-First World War years. (NAS/BRB(Residuary)Ltd)

proud and where a royal occasion could be held.

Even the improved facilities at Waverley were stretched when the season for excursions and holidays came round. Prior to the First World War, a majority of the working population received two weeks' unpaid leave per year. At the Edinburgh Trades' Holiday some 60,000 people were estimated to take a train from Waverley. At this peak 'resources were severely taxed and relief trains were run' – the NBR had some 600 carriages available though some were 'ramshackle'. Although taking time off work for a day trip meant no pay, railway excursions continued to have much appeal with such trips giving a sense of adventure. Cycling had become a craze and some families going to 'summer quarters' had seven or eight 'bikes' to load in addition to cases, hampers and trunks. This kept station staff, especially porters, very busy and they could earn plenty of 'tips'.

The new North British Station Hotel displayed two large paintings near its entrance that depicted 'War' and 'Peace'. During its construction, the South African War had been fought between 1898 and 1900. There were heavy casualties in this colonial conflict and an impressive war memorial was placed on the new North Bridge. Much worse was to come with the Great War of 1914-18. Tensions between Britain and the German Empire had been increasing with bitter rivalries on the high seas and in Africa. In 1909 the Royal Naval Dockyard was established at Rosyth to support the Home Fleet, and Redford Barracks was constructed for the army, augmenting the garrison at Edinburgh Castle. Both military and naval

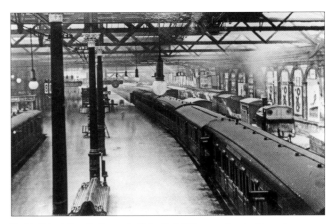

The Up Main platform looking west with the North Wall covered in advertisements. (T.Harden Collection)

personnel, plus 'Territorials' going to summer camps, were seen in transit through Waverley Station.

In 1912 the government formed a Railway Executive Committee from the general managers of the main companies. Its purpose was to co-ordinate railway services in the event of war. The government would then take control of the railways using the existing managements to carry out its policies. For the North British, the conflict that began on 4 August 1914 immediately intensified its freight and special traffic, caused many express and other services to be withdrawn and reduced its supplies of essential materials. Territorial regiments were mobilised and on a Sunday that month seventy troop trains went through Waverley Station. Railway employees joined up

The view from a vantage point at Jacob's Ladder in 1913 shows the east side of Waverley Station with (left to right) the goods yard, signal box, extensive sidings and Calton Road. (Science & Society Picture Library)

The new North Bridge with cable tramcars, the North British Station Hotel and the extensive west roof of the new station in 1903. (Author's Collection)

in such numbers that an embargo had to be placed on them doing so – otherwise the system could not have been run.

With numerous troop trains leaving Edinburgh, Waverley Station became a place of tearful farewells. . In November 1914 a buffet for troops was set up, the first in the country; with volunteers assisting day and night; by 1919 over 2 million meals had been served to troops at Waverley. Due to the threat of possible invasion, the East Coast was considered vulnerable and railwaymen were warned that all means of transport were to be removed or destroyed if instructions were issued to that effect. With so many troops and war workers in transit, access to platforms was further tightened at British stations.

Far from being 'over by Christmas' the conflict continued for four years and the losses were devastating. At Waverley, the North British set aside a Red Cross rest room for the sick and

wounded which is commemorated in a plaque. City infirmaries were supplemented by many military and auxiliary hospitals and several railway companies provided hospital trains. The NBR supported a Red Cross depot where medical supplies, bedding and knitted 'comforts' were packed for despatch by rail. It also gave twenty-five locomotives for service in France, one of which, *Maude* (named after a general) is preserved in the Scottish Railway Museum at Bo'ness.

On 2 April 1916, the conflict came close when there was a Zeppelin raid on Edinburgh. A number of incendiary and high explosive bombs were dropped from the airship that did considerable damage to property and caused casualties. Although there were explosions in East Princes Street Gardens and at Haymarket, the railway remained intact. By January 1917 the war economy and shortage of manpower caused the temporary closure of some stations, among them Craigmillar and Piershill, and some passenger services were curtailed.

In 1914, when war broke out, the employees of the North British Railway numbered 24,625 but one out of every five enlisted. When peace came in November 1918 one in every sixteen of these had been lost. In March 1922, a bronze war memorial carrying 775 names was dedicated at Waverley Station to record the sacrifice and honour the memory of these North British men. It was placed on the east wall of the Booking Hall but is now displayed on the south wall of the main building.

There would be no 'going back to normal' for the railways or for Waverley Station in the post-war years. An era was at an end, and with a generation gone and survivors often impaired, uncertain times had begun.

Overlooked by Calton Jail, shunting engines await their turn beside the imposing signal gantry at Waverley East. A water column is on the right. (M. Boakes/A.G. Ellis)

Through Troubled Years

Throughout the years of the First World War, the railway companies had been under government direction and run as one entity. There were arguments for maintaining state control. Was this the time to buy out the private companies? Union opinion favoured 'nationalisation' but for most managements and shareholders this was a step too far.

When peace came in November 1918, the railways were sorely depleted, maintenance had been deferred and investment had dried up. The government proposed a scheme of amalgamation for the private railway companies, the intention being to 'secure economy of operation and increase efficiency of administration'. The North British Railway board considered the move unconstitutional – stating that it was 'impossible to suggest a greater violation of the rights of British subjects'. It was argued that the five Scottish lines should form one system but the Railway Companies' Association was unable to resolve the matter of compensation for each company. A Railways Act of 1921, effective from 1 January 1923, enforced 'a systematic, compulsory amalgamation scheme', devised by the government, on thirty-seven private railway companies in Britain.

The grouping into the 'Big Four' – the Great Western, the London & North Eastern (LNER), the London, Midland & Scottish (LMS) and the Southern – followed, but there would be no 'Scottish Railways'. The dominance of the East and West Coast lines in Britain's transport system was thought so significant that, as far as Scotland was concerned, two companies emerged – the LNER, focussing on the East Coast route and absorbing the North British and the Great North of Scotland Railways, while the LMSR on the West Coast, combined the Caledonian, Glasgow & South Western and the Highland Railways. Waverley Station became part of the LNER.

The transition to what was seen as 'London control' was far from welcome among Scottish railwaymen. For many, the old North British – in spite of its faults – was more than a job, it was a way of life. It was not unusual for fifty years' service to be given to a railway company and loyalty could be intense. Instructions now came from south of the border; there were new policies, new methods of working and new uniforms. Out went the 'bronze green' paint for passenger locomotives and the claret coaches of the North British. The locomotives and carriages had new liveries – apple green for passenger engines, black for the rest; coaching stock was varnished teak. There were however new opportunities when former NBR drivers at Haymarket had to 'learn the road' to Newcastle and work expresses on the East Coast main line. However, Waverley Station and its operation remained much the same.

There was some satisfaction when William Whitelaw, the former North British chairman, was given the same position in the LNER. Described as 'astute, enterprising and tactful', he held that appointment until 1938. The LNER had a decentralised approach to governance that gave Scotland a general manager and a local board of directors. Sadly, the new company, though covering a large area, was economically weak. In the 1920s and 1930s, its industrial heartland in the North East of England, dependent on coal mining, iron and steel and heavy industry, was a seriously depressed area. In 1923 the LNER was the leading coal railway in Britain hauling over 100 million tons, but such tonnages were in sharp decline

Above left: The LNER 'Art Deco' logo.

Below left: The former North British 4-4-2 named Waverley, now LNER No.9876, on LNER coaches at Waverley West. (Author's Collection)

Below right: Former North Eastern locomotives continued to haul East Coast expresses in the early 1920s. (J.L. Stevenson Collection)

This view of Princes Street shows electric tramcars and motor vehicles that increasingly took traffic away from rail services in the inter-war years. (Author's Collection)

and this would hit its revenue streams hard.

In 1926 came the General Strike when the whole country came to a standstill. Some railwaymen with the assistance of volunteers tried to keep a limited train service running. After just nine days, the strike fizzled out but the miners stayed 'out' for months and coal became scarce. In the aftermath, the LNER was forced to reduce staff numbers – employees retained had to accept cuts of 2½ per cent in salaries and wages, and no increase for two years.

The post-grouping companies were dominated by directors and managements for whom out-competing rival railways had been a basic philosophy, underpinning the provision of both passenger and freight services. Now the railways were being challenged by new transport modes – the motorcar, bus and lorry. For the South Suburban route out of Waverley, competition only became tougher when in 1922 Edinburgh Corporation's new electric tramcars, supplied from overhead wires, began running. The tram system soon made serious inroads into 'South Sub' services.

Worse was to follow. Although motorbuses had first

'The Flying Scotsman' heads north with the Gresley designed 4-6-2 of that name at the head of the train – a publicity postcard by the LNER. (Author's Collection)

appeared on Edinburgh streets in 1914, there had been big technological advances in motor vehicles in the First World War when servicemen became familiar with their operation and maintenance. War surplus lorries enabled veterans to set up garages and, being exempt from rail freight pricing, their lower charges stole goods traffic from the railways. Buses with cheaper fares, better frequencies and more flexible routes, took business away from rural lines. At Waverley Station, hansom cabs, with their horsey smell, had already been replaced by motor taxis, giving off petrol fumes and smoky exhausts as they puttered up and down the ramps.

Moreover, the LNER was burdened with secondary and branch lines that failed to make money. From the early 1920s, closures of stations and cessations of passenger services followed, including some served by trains from Waverley – such as Granton (1925), Gogar and Turnhouse (1930), or the branches to Gullane (1932), to Dolphinton (1933) and to Gifford and Glencorse (1933). It was cost saving, reducing the wages bill as passenger stations by law required three staff – stationmaster, booking clerk and porter. Nevertheless, Whitelaw and the LNER board were at pains to keep lines open for freight in the hope of an upturn in trade.

From a passenger perspective, the interwar years brought little betterment to Waverley Station other than minimal repairs, routine coats of paint and the use of the sweeping brush. In 1923 a letter to *The Scotsman* had offered a suggestion for improvement – escalators should replace 'the wretched Waverley Steps'. Edinburgh Corporation's Town Clerk asked the City Engineer to report on installing 'a moving staircase' and Waygood-Otis Ltd was invited to produce a scheme. Waygood were lift pioneers in Britain while Otis dominated elevator construction in the United States. Like the London Underground installations, those at Waverley would have been electrically powered with 'a weather proof enclosure over the whole escalator'. They could have carried 4,000 people an hour and two sets would have cost £17,000. But there was a problem – Edinburgh Corporation did not own the Waverley Steps – it was the cash-strapped LNER, and that company declined to make such an investment.

Nevertheless, the LNER promoted fast trains and luxury travel. Even in its relatively impoverished condition, the board had aspirations – speed and comfort. While the company struggled to pay dividends, from its works in Doncaster and Darlington, Nigel Gresley, its talented Chief Mechanical Engineer, with his teams, produced locomotives that broke speed records and trains that caught the public imagination. (For medical reasons, he was born in Edinburgh and is commemorated in a plaque within Waverley Station).

In 1922 Gresley had designed a large locomotive with 4-6-2 wheel arrangement for the Great Northern Railway. This Pacific type became the core of the LNER's 'big engine' policy to handle fast but increasingly heavy trains on the East Coast services. In 1924, a new engine No.1472, built at Doncaster,

The east end of Waverley with its smoke-stained frontage and signal gantry – a former NER Atlantic locomotive is on the right. (Science & Society Picture Library)

was given the name *Flying Scotsman* and exhibited by the LNER at the Empire Exhibition at Wembley. The former 'Special Scotch Express', the 10am train from Kings Cross, was renamed 'The Flying Scotsman' and the publicity conscious LNER published a booklet about it. (Haymarket shed is said to have made a headboard for the locomotive, similar to the NBR versions – just painted cast iron). Sister engines followed, and to emphasise speed, they received the names of racehorse winners of the Derby and the Oaks.

A description of Waverley Station in 1926 shows just how capacious it was – its platforms being capable of handling 23 trains at one time with the long 'Up' and 'Down' Mains each accommodating two trains simultaneously. With all platforms now 'gated', platform tickets – costing one penny and valid

for one hour – had to be bought. Although platform indicators continued in use, particular platforms were allocated to certain train routes 'to ease passenger anxieties'. Except for 'a few hours on Sundays', the division and marshalling of trains made Waverley a busy place. Typically, staff dealt with 1,000 trains every 24 hours with four shunting engines being employed, often all at one time. Three 'terminal spurs' beside Waverley

Below left: The 'Queen of Scots Pullman', introduced by the LNER in 1928, is seen in Princes Street Gardens hauled by the former NBR 4-4-2 LNER No.9877 Liddesdale. (Science & Society Picture Gallery)

Below right: When the LNER introduced third class sleeping cars, the 'Night Scotsman' running to and from Waverley Station was popular. (Author's Collection)

THE NIGHT SCOTSMAN
Leaves King's Cross nightly at 10.25.

Market were used for storing stock. With restaurant and sleeping cars on the principal expresses to be shunted, there might also be through coaches for Southampton or Penzance, and fish vans to attach. It was a time when much goods traffic, such as perishables and other special consignments, were conveyed by vans on passenger trains.

The Waverley day began with the arrival between 3 and 4.30am of the sleeping car expresses from London that had to change engines and leave passengers for Edinburgh. 'The Aberdonian' was the long sleeping car express from Kings Cross to Aberdeen. O.S.Nock, the railway author, described the 'eerie solitude' in the great station as the train drew in at four in the morning. There were sleepers for Inverness and Fort William to shunt and fresh engines to attach. From 6am came a succession of night trains including sleepers from St. Pancras via the Waverley Route; this also had through coaches, including one from Bristol. Only between 11pm and 4am was the station empty and quiet.

By morning, there was a peak of activity on the 'Up' side at Waverley with 'The Flying Scotsman' express setting off at 10am. Soon expresses for St.Pancras and the popular Pullman car train for Harrogate left. Throughout the day a succession of local trains arrived and departed at the dock platforms at either end of the station. Some were also named and carried headboards – the 'Lothian Coast Express' to North Berwick, and the 'Fifeshire Coast Express' to St.Andrews, being examples. Expresses also ran to and from Glasgow and Aberdeen.

Extra pressures came in summer when at the 'month's end', many holidaymakers took up or left their summer quarters at the coast or in the Highlands. However, day trips could still see as many as 56,000 passengers being conveyed out and back from Waverley. The station staff, now numbering some 400, included the Chief Station Master with his three assistants, inspectors, clerks, foremen, guards, shunters, pointsmen, ticket collectors, porters, lampmen, empty carriage attendants, carriage cleaners, waiting room attendants, gatekeepers and office cleaners. There were 32 signalmen. Young lads were employed to register trains and to assist with lamps. The

Booking Office staff of 25 had their own manager, as did the Parcels Agent with his 32 clerks and 77 porters. The Goods Agent also had a staff of similar size to that at the main station. In overall authority was the LNER's Passenger Manager for the 'South Scottish Area' with his office at Waterloo Place.

So far the 8¼ hour agreement of 1895 for the Edinburgh-London run still held. However, the 1928 summer timetable announced that 'The Flying Scotsman' would go non-stop from Kings Cross to Waverley, a distance of 392.9 miles. The route was now equipped with water troughs whereby supplies could be picked up by tender scoops while running, and the engines also had corridor tenders making a crew change possible en route. Speed was again the lure and the LNER would excel in its attainment, but comfort and fashion were not overlooked – a cocktail bar and a barber's shop were on board. The company publicity machine ensured that the press took note. Fast rail services were a boon to businessmen and civil servants going 'up to London'.

That year 'The Queen of Scots Pullman' first ran between Kings Cross and Glasgow Queen Street via Edinburgh Waverley, and although a supplement had to be paid, it was popular. The LNER's powerful engines were also being complemented by more new coaches with higher standards of passenger amenity – there were now restaurant cars for both first and third-class passengers. In 1928 third-class sleeping cars were introduced with four berths to a compartment and a pillow and rug per passenger – at long last 'thirds' could lie down overnight. Consequently, 'The Night Scotsman' became so popular that it ran in three portions at peak holiday times.

The hopes of better economic conditions were dashed in 1929 with the Wall Street crash. This plunged Britain into financial chaos, causing industrial shut downs and prolonged unemployment in Scotland and the North of England. It became the Great Depression. Notwithstanding licensing restrictions placed on road haulage in 1933, rail freight continued to decrease and the private railway companies were brought perilously close to bankruptcy.

The Edinburgh district suffered less than areas of heavy industry as it was the seat of government with the Scottish Office and had a large civil service establishment. Banking, financial and legal services were major activities and the city was a cultural hub. It also had many industries producing consumer goods from breweries and bakeries (biscuits were a speciality), to distilling, papermaking, printing and publishing. All this acted as an economic cushion. Its business communities and professional citizens were judged 'comfortably off' and owning a motorcar was a widely held ambition. Cars, once custom built and very expensive, became 'affordable' with Austin, Morris and other makes rolling off southern production

Left: The LNER brought the Director class 4-4-0s to Scotland, giving the engines Scottish names and placing them on local services. (Author's Collection)

In the 1930s new LNER Pacific locomotives became familiar on expresses to and from Waverley for Glasgow, Perth, Dundee and Aberdeen. (J.L Stevenson Collection)

lines by the thousand. So many motorcars were appearing on Edinburgh's streets that in 1929 it was suggested that the roof of Waverley Station should be converted into a giant car park. The Town Council also discussed the location for a bus station and an aerodrome to serve the city.

In tough times, the LNER's marketing department fought to retain passengers. Whitelaw favoured the naming of passenger locomotives – believing this encouraged an interest in railways. Such enthusiasm was apparent at Waverley Station. Some engine classes sent to Scotland, following North British practice, were given names from the Waverley novels and others from Scottish history. For viewing the new engines, the bridges across the tracks in Princes Street Gardens were good vantage points but even better were the fences in the gardens themselves. Edinburgh parents took their families to watch the trains from

there, a free entertainment for generations of the city's children.

Tourism continued for the better off and Waverley's passengers were remembered as 'well dressed and mannered'. To attract their business, the LNER produced memorable posters – of Edinburgh Castle, the Scott Monument and the Forth Bridge.

It also devised the 'Northern Belle', an excursion train that toured its Scottish lines, including the Waverley Route, taking passengers to 'See the Beauties of Scotland in Comfort' for

Below left: A publicity postcard for the North British Station Hotel, a popular venue in Edinburgh in LNER years. (Author's Collection)

Below: A LNER Coronation train with A4 No.4491 Commonwealth of Australia draws crowds at Waverley in 1937. (A.E. Glen Collection)

Telegrams – BRITISH, EDINBURGH.
Telephones – 8966-8972 Central.

NORTH BRITISH STATION HOTEL Edinburgh

The Coronation train, hauled by No. 4489 Dominion of Canada, heads north on the East Coast route to Edinburgh. (Author's Collection)

seven days. With first-class rail accommodation, and meals 'all in', it cost £20. Meanwhile, the 'North British Station Hotel', with its name now in neon lights, continued to be popular. For the less well off, the LNER offered 'Rambles' Cards' at Waverley to encourage the new activity of hiking, while two-day excursion tickets to Fort William were aimed at climbers tackling Ben Nevis.

In spite of their apparent rivalry, the LNER and LMS were aware of each other's plans for Anglo-Scottish services as information was generally shared – with the LNER trying to keep ahead of the game even in years when its revenue was falling. By 1935 it launched its 'Silver Jubilee' train for which the locomotives were 'top secret' until revealed as streamlined A4 class engines in silver livery. 'Steamlining' was the result of wind tunnel tests. The A4s were soon reeling off the miles from London to Newcastle at 90mph and one was tested north to Edinburgh Waverley covering the difficult 124 miles in 114 minutes. In 1937 more streamliners in 'garter blue' (and named after the Empire's major countries) were built for the 'Coronation' train. This had a six-hour schedule between Kings Cross and Waverley with passengers again paying a

supplement to travel in its air-conditioned 'Art Deco' coaches.

In Edinburgh, such trains created a spectacle that drew crowds at the east end of Waverley Station. An observer recalled:-

'As the minutes went bye – the time showing on the North British Hotel clock… the white exhaust from the great engine rose against the smoke-stained station façade … then a whistle shrilled, the green flag waved, the engine answered with its throaty chime, and amid the roar of steam, the train began moving… Soon the last coach was disappearing into the tunnel at Calton Hill and the drama was over…'

But there was a problem. There had been protest in Edinburgh from the 1920s when the LNER announced that it would charge three pence for a platform ticket at Waverley instead of one penny. People resented having to pay to meet passengers from trains or to see them off. By 1938, with the attraction of the 'Coronation' train, the streamliners and other new engines, crowd management and safety were concerns. It was explained that 'multiple marshalling' took place at Waverley Station – complex shunting movements carried out in tight time frames. The LNER would have preferred to admit only people actually travelling to its Waverley platforms – hence the 3d charge as a deterrent – but it was also a source of some revenue in hard times.

A major investment that the LNER did make at Waverley Station was new colour light signalling. Negotiations began with the Bank of Scotland in February 1935 with a view to replacing the West Signal Box close to the Mound Tunnel. As the bank had successfully intervened to prevent structures being erected within its view, its directors had 'no intention of abandoning their right of controlling the nature of buildings west of Waverley Bridge'. However, Edinburgh Corporation thought a niche in the gardens would be a convenient place for a signal box. This 'niche' was not Bank of Scotland ground at all, yet a firm line was taken by it over the 'position, extent, elevation and construction of the new signal box'. Edinburgh Corporation then asked the LNER for 'a lavatory for the bowling green' behind the new building and further unsettled the bank.

'Waverley West', with its 227 miniature levers, was brought into use in October 1936, but not without hitches causing train delays. It is remembered as a miserable place to work – its lack of height gave poor visibility and much exposure to steam, smoke and fumes coming from the Mound Tunnel. A new East Signal Box near Calton Tunnel followed in 1938. At both locations, there was extensive track circuiting and 'multiple aspect colour light signals', plus platform route indicators and 'train describing equipment'.

The Bank of Scotland would have liked all redundant structures removed, but the railway had other ideas. The bases of the old signal boxes became shunters' mess rooms. In and

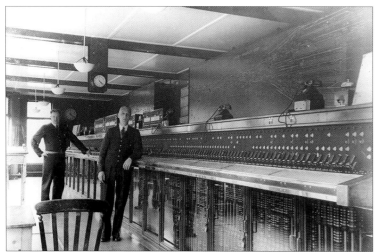

The interior of Waverley East signal box that had a colour light signalling system installed in 1938. (David Hey Collection)

around Waverley, linesmen's bothies, workshops, paint and sawdust stores, electrical plant rooms and the like, were tucked away in odd corners. However, new accommodation was also found for staff canteens.

In step with these developments, the platforms at Waverley were renumbered to make them easier for passengers to find. Previously, the four principal through platforms had been known as 'Main Up, east end', 'Main Down, east end' and the same for the west end – without numbers. These became 'Nos. 1,10,11 and 19' respectively. So the platforms were now 1 to 10 at the east end and from 11 to 19 at the west end to reduce passenger confusion. According to LNER practice, the numbers appeared above the platforms in white on blue panels. In 1938 loudspeakers 'for directing passengers and making announcements as the occasion arises' were installed; this 'sound equipment' (a microphone in a box) would shortly prove invaluable. Soon the station's wall hung signal boxes found new uses – latterly, becoming announcers' cabins conveniently overlooking the main lines with the ladies remembered for their Edinburgh versions of BBC English.

Goods and parcels traffic had felt the impact of the economic downturn but changes were taking place in this sector too. Advertisements now read, ' Send your goods by road rail container', a demountable system of which the railways were proud. Similar facilities were also available for household removals. Extra fast deliveries by 'Green Arrow', an express freight service, were introduced for which the LNER named a locomotive of the V2 class. The extensive goods yard at Waverley with its range of sidings continued to serve fruit and vegetable merchants and famously 'The Scotsman' newspaper offices. The latter's sidings were lengthy and

tucked under buildings in Market Street, described as an 'undercroft'. With brick piers and steel girders, it was not elegant but practical, a symptom of the lack of space which typified the station. The parcels office, in neo-classical style, still stood on the Waverley Bridge.

Faced with continuing competition for freight, the railway companies again argued for 'a level playing field' with road haulage, and in 1938 launched their campaign for 'A Square Deal'. This asked for reform to free railways from regulated charges, allowing them to set their own rates. Though accepted by the government of the day, the international situation and imminent conflict caused a deferral.

The Second World War began on 3 September 1939 and immediately the railways came under government control. A new Executive Committee was set up to operate the companies as a unit. All signage that might assist an invader was removed from stations and troop trains were given top priority. The mass exodus of children from cities likely to be under aerial attack began and Waverley Station had its share of the Scottish trains that over three days carried 178,543 evacuees to safe rural locations. In November 1939 a canteen for service personnel was opened at Waverley and was staffed by volunteers; while it was 'free' to troops, it was dependent on donations from the public.

The LNER had prepared emergency headquarters, located in the old Scotland Street tunnel and fitted out with offices, telephone lines and welfare facilities. Its Scottish services would have been run from there in the event of disruptions at Waverley or other places on the system. The tunnel also provided an air raid shelter in central Edinburgh. Fear of aerial bombardment had been heightened by the attempted attack

In the interests of economy, the LMS and LNER did joint advertising – here for Edinburgh with Waverley Bridge in view and a train in Princes Street Gardens. (Author's Collection)

Above: The John Menzies bookstall at Waverley just prior to the Second World War.
(Edinburgh & Glasgow Railway Guidebook)
Below: The interior of Scotland Street tunnel showing the emergency headquarters
prepared by the LNER. (Nick Catford)

Bottom: From the Mound tunnel, V2 2-6-2 BR No.60931 heads a passenger train in the
latter 1950s. (John Robertson)

on Rosyth Naval Dockyard on 16 October 1939 – the first such assault in Britain during the Second World War.

Before the outbreak, preparations were made for civil defence training in which staff at Waverley Station took part. In the station, lights were dimmed but switched off entirely if air raid sirens sounded. Air raid precaution (ARP) wardens patrolled the streets to ensure that no lights were visible. Fire watching for incendiary bombs became routine, with volunteers positioned by night on the station roof. Sand bags protected station entrances. Waverley's prize-winning ambulance team practised its first aid and stretcher routines while other employees took on fire fighting and rescue duties. Everyone carried a gas mask. Although some railway stations had the glass in their roofs removed, this was not done at Waverley – the roof was simply too extensive. With soot from above, plus smoke and steam from below, the glass would be effectively 'blacked out' in any case. Office windows were protected from shattering with gummed paper strips. Waverley was also within view of the garrison at Edinburgh Castle and its guns.

Leith and Granton as port areas were targeted in a 'mini-blitz' of April 1941 when the Abbeyhill area was also attacked and peppered with incendiaries. An attempt to hit the railway lines out of Waverley was off target, but a bomb made a crater in the lawn at Holyrood Palace. Later both Edinburgh and Leith were subjected to 'hit and run' raids. Railway yards and depots were very vulnerable and instructions were given to limit glare from the fire doors of steam locomotives that might reveal their position.

Civilian travel was discouraged with posters asking, 'Is Your Journey Really Necessary?' Few 'non-essential' trains ran and

those that did were very congested. They became lengthy and slow – 'The Flying Scotsman' might take nine hours or longer to and from Waverley. As time passed, people were permitted to travel to the countryside to help on farms producing food for the nation. With petrol rationed and private cars 'laid up' in garages, passenger numbers actually went up. In advance of D-Day, the invasion of Europe on 6 June 1944, numerous troop trains and goods vehicles carrying munitions and equipment

Top left: Conveying mail was a major activity at Waverley and V2 BR No.60824 prepares for the Borders route. Roof panels have been removed to allow smoke to escape. (David Bain)
Top right: Princes Street Gardens were popular vantage points for watching trains; here J38 0-6-0 BR No.65907 leaves with a local train. (Author's Collection)
Right: British Railways decision to 'stick with steam' produced new locomotive classes. Here 2-6-4T BR No.80113 awaits the signal at Waverley West. (Author's Collection)

The east frontage of Waverley with A4 BR No.60031 Golden Plover setting off with an East Coast express. (Author's Collection)

Inter-city diesel multiple units (DMUs), Swindon built, were introduced on the Edinburgh-Glasgow route in 1957. (Author's Collection)

passed through Edinburgh, some of them via Waverley.

When VE Day came in May 1945, the railways were in a seriously rundown condition. Nevertheless, for Christmas that year, the LNER introduced 'a festive and picturesque innovation' at Waverley. This was a Christmas tree, the first at any railway station in Scotland. The General Manager switched on the fairy lights and money was collected for local hospitals.

With the railway system having been managed as one unit in wartime, there was now a strong case for continuing to do so. 'Nationalisation', or state ownership of the means of production, was Labour Party policy and in July 1945 that party was swept to power in the first post-war election. Accordingly, in January 1948 the private railway companies became state-owned as British Railways, part of an integrated transport system with road haulage and buses. What would Waverley Station's future be? Years of austerity and rationing lay ahead.

The railways were now dependent on central government for funding, appointments and strategy under a British Transport Commission, and they had a duty to pay their way taking one year with another. Overall management, however, was in the hands of the Rail Executive. A Scottish Region

emerged and 'Caledonian blue' was chosen for its new station signs or 'totems'. At Waverley Station, an indication of 'getting back to normal' was the reappearance of the 'Queen of Scots' Pullman in 1948. However, that August disastrous floods on the East Coast line swept bridges away and washed out tracks. For months station staff had to cope with re-scheduled services using the Waverley route until the East Coast line could be re-opened.

By the early 1950s, Waverley Station was a busy place for staff. At the morning rush hour, it was 'standing room only' in the timekeeper's office as the night shift signed off and day turns signed on. The assistant stationmaster and his inspectors, departmental foremen, carriage cleaning staff and ticket collectors, were there awaiting 'news' of the northbound night services. Brian Farish, then a junior clerk, recalled telegraph messages coming 'thick and fast' and telephones ringing – both GPO and omnibus circuits, often all at once:-

'That morning there was bad news from Craigentinny – a defective coach had been taken off, playing havoc with seat reservations. Then Control called …the 10.35pm from Kings Cross was running an hour late and holding up the Night Scotsman … Soon the West signal box came on the 'phone, 'We've got a points failure at the Mound Tunnel – everything's going out north side'. So it went on and on, week in week out.' Waverley staff had to be adaptable and resilient.

Although there were proposals for electrification in 1951, the Rail Executive preferred to 'stick with steam', a proven technology using UK coal. So new 'Standard' locomotive classes were designed and all steel rolling stock. Already BR was losing ground to long distance coach travel on potentially profitable trunk routes. In 1953 it fought back with 'Starlight Specials', overnight trains to and from London with competitive fares. The Coronation that year saw the 'Elizabethan Express' launched. This was a non-stop revival, hauled mainly by A4 streamliners between Kings Cross and Waverley, which excited rail watchers and won fame in a documentary film. Meanwhile, the youthful hobby of 'train spotting' was booming and there

Left: DMUs were soon running on other routes from Waverley – this Gloucester Carriage & Wagon example served Fife stations. (Author's Collection)
Below: Diesel locomotives also appeared in the 1950s – this Type 4 (later Class 40) carries a 'Heart of Midlothian' headboard. (Author's Collection)

were many engine classes to be seen at Waverley Station.

With passenger numbers shrinking, some local services were reduced and others had already been abandoned – to Dalkeith(1942) and to North Leith (1947). The Haddington branch closed to passengers in 1949, Polton, Penicuik and Ratho in 1951, Leith Central shut in 1952, Bathgate services went in 1956, and more would follow. These closures told on Waverley Station, and according to old hands, it was 'not the place it had been'. In 1957 its lighting was renewed (not before time) and a year later, the Jeffrey Street footbridge was shut 'pending repairs' but its closure was soon permanent.

Until 1955 BR was profitable, then its finances became problematic. With a Conservative government in power, BTC had announced its 'Modernisation Plan' to update the ageing rail network and rolling stock. Substantial investment over fifteen years was proposed with a switch from steam to diesel or electric traction. Trials of diesel multiple units (DMUs) took place in 1956 – the year when 'third class' became 'second'. An innovation in 1960 was 'Motorail', offering a daytime service for passengers and their cars between Waverley and Kings Cross. Platforms at Waverley's east end were adapted by infilling for parking, loading and unloading vehicles.

In 1957 an express service of intercity DMUs, built at Swindon, had been introduced between Edinburgh Waverley and Glasgow Queen Street. These were a sensation allowing passengers to travel in much cleaner conditions. A year later Gloucester Class 100 DMUs displaced steam haulage on Edinburgh and Lothian routes while Metro-Cammell Class 101s appeared in Fife. On 8 September 1961 the last timetabled non-stop run from Kings Cross to Waverley was hauled by the legendary engine BR No.60022 *Mallard* , the world speed record holder for steam traction. DMUs were tried on the South Suburban route without attracting much custom and in 1962 its stations closed.

Prototype diesel locomotives were appearing, some having questionable reliability and others a poor power-to-weight ratio. However, a speculative venture by English Electric in 1955 produced the classic Deltic locomotive, and following its success BR's Eastern Region ordered production versions that were introduced in 1961. Their six-hour schedules on the East Coast main line were thrilling and they had names – of racehorses and regiments. A handful came to Haymarket depot and Waverley Station soon echoed to their powerful roar.

The Transport Act of 1962 established the British Railways Board with Richard Beeching, a former industrial chemist at ICI, as a board member. Pressure was on 'to make the railways pay' and in 1963 his report, '*The Reshaping of British Railways*' identified the profitable businesses for rail as the intercity routes and long distance freight. The report recommended station closures, the cutting of secondary routes and the elimination of stopping services. The 'Beeching Axe' made headline news and there were strong objections

A Deltic locomotive BR No.55017 The Durham Light Infantry leaves with the Flying Scotsman from the old Up Main platform. (Author's Collection)

from many communities. Even before the cuts, there were further closures – at Peebles (1962) and Musselburgh (1964).

By this time, BR passenger numbers had fallen to a low point of 630 million a year. The famed Waverley Route through the Borders to Carlisle and the Glenfarg line were under threat, while Princes Street Station, Edinburgh's other key terminus, was shut in 1965 with its services transferring to Waverley. That year BR became 'British Rail', with a new corporate identity, a 'double arrow logo' and new uniforms for staff – but this concealed low morale in the industry.

In 1964 when goods traffic at Waverley Station ceased, the yard was soon cleared and made into a car park. The rundown continued with service withdrawals on the Waverley

Above: With traffic in decline, the route through Princes Street Gardens was redesigned in the 1980s; here a Class 24 locomotive is on a ballast train. (Author's Collection)
Below: The sorry state of the former South Suburban platforms in August 1979 with a Class 20 locomotive on a works train. (J.L. Stevenson)

Route and for stopping trains to Berwick, plus the abandonment of more branches in the southeast. Waverley's once bustling east end was almost deserted and one diesel shunting locomotive sufficed.

In the Transport Act of 1968, Barbara Castle, the Labour Minister of Transport, removed the quantitative restrictions on road haulage, introduced to protect the railways in 1933. This only made competition tougher in this sector. However, it was recognised that some lines were 'socially necessary but unremunerative' and hence deserving of subsidy. The Waverley Route, a possible contender, had hung on until 6 January 1969 when, amid bitter protests, the last passenger train ran.

In 1970 the Commonwealth Games were held at Edinburgh and this was the cue for Waverley Station to be 'modernised'. Its distinctive octagonal booking office was dismantled and replaced by a 'travel centre' on the south side; the carved friezes were concealed with plain stone facings and the bronze statue went. Oak panelling, the decorative clock and even the war memorial were removed. The north side became a food court. The mosaic floor was lost under dark terrazzo. Glass-fronted units displaced the original kiosks on the west concourse. Not surprisingly, the 'refurbishment and modernisation' was judged 'unsympathetic' – the modern and the *belle époque* did not co-exist successfully.

In May 1971, a service upgrade was advertised – Class 27s on 'push-pull' trains of six coaches would take over the Edinburgh-Glasgow runs and their journey times of 43 to 45 minutes have never been bettered. Another breakthrough was

1: Push-pull systems were used on Edinburgh-Glasgow services in the 1970s and 1980s. BR No.47706 Strathclyde is seen on such a train in June 1984. (Author's Collection)

2: The north side at Waverley – looking west towards former carriage sidings – shows a Class 47 BR No. 47420 on a train in 1978. (Author's Collection)

3: When BR's new High Speed Trains (HSTs) began running in the 1970s, they could soon be observed from Princes Street Gardens. (Bruce Peter).

4: A panel on the north wall marked the entrance to the Scotland Street tunnel. (J.L. Stevenson)

5: Happy times in 1986 when the Scottish Railway Preservation Society ran 'Santa Specials' round the 'South Sub' with NBR No.673 Maude. (Ann Glen)

when the Inter-City 125s appeared at Waverley. A British Rail design, these thoroughly modern, good-looking trains relied on two factors that the LNER had promoted so successfully – speed and comfort. This was 'The Age of the Train' and passenger numbers soared. In 1979 the fastest 'Flying Scotsman' ever covered the journey to Edinburgh in 4 hours 37minutes. The 125s still run, notably forming the 'Highland Chieftain' from Kings Cross via Waverley to Inverness and on East Coast services to Aberdeen.

In 1976 a new signal power box in modernist style was built on the south margin of the former goods yard. This made Waverley's surviving signal boxes redundant. Adjustments to platform ends and tracks, modifications that had been ongoing since the 1930s, continued but the old suburban platforms were now rarely used and fell into decay. With steam haulage gone, in the latter 1970s the main building at Waverley was stone cleaned. The removal of grime brought a new awareness to the worth of Victorian architecture and the station was seen afresh for its architectural and historic interest.

In 1980, Class 47 locomotives with driving brake second opens (DBSOs) came to the Edinburgh-Glasgow runs, reputedly the only services on the Scottish network that made money. Under Chris Green, a dynamic General Manager, the brand name 'ScotRail' was coined. When the platform barriers were removed at Waverley in 1984, it became an 'open' station. That year a metal clad Royal Mail depot was placed on the site of former platforms on the east side – the first of an unhappy assortment of structures to be inserted within Waverley's train shed. The

balustrades on Waverley Bridge were closed off with fibreglass units, thereby hiding the station even more from the public. The old information office, a strategic advertisement for the railway on the bridge, became a wine bar and the former parcels office on the south corner, an enquiry bureau for Lothian Buses. The railway's presence, its *persona*, seemed to be in retreat.

In an attempt to reduce subsidy levels, railway land and other assets was being sold off. First the hotels went. In 1983 Edinburgh's North British Hotel, a key element in the city's social scene for decades, was sold and its links with Waverley Station ceased. New owners Trusthouse Forte tried to maintain the reputation of 'the N.B.' and to revive its 'tired' décor. Subsequently the company lost control in a hostile takeover bid and in 1990 it was re-named 'The Balmoral'. Only in 1997 did Sir Rocco Forte resume ownership and after closure and refurbishment, the hotel re-emerged as a five star establishment.

In 1986 a glass-clad operations office for train crew and a catering services building were completed at Waverley. The station's east concourse was now likened to an industrial estate dominated by servicing facilities and vehicle movements. Structures proliferated on the west side too – among them a 'brick and panel' office for the British Transport Police and a plant and services facility. North of the main building, a line of retail outlets of no architectural merit was opened.

Despite 'above inflation' increases in fares and determined efforts to cut costs in the 1980s, there was difficulty in securing

Top left: The John Menzies bookstall after 'modernisation' prior to the Commonwealth Games in 1970. (Edinburgh & Glasgow Railway Guidebook)
Bottom left: The retail invasion on Waverley's north concourse was seen as a 'cheap and cheerful' opportunity in the 1980s. (C. Naples/Stevenson Collection)
Top right: With a new signalling centre (right) and the goods shed abandoned, the decrepit 'South Sub' platforms and station roof as seen in 1983. (C. Naples/Stevenson Collection)
Bottom right: The glass-clad Operations Centre on the east concourse in 1986. (C. Naples/Stevenson Collection)

adequate government funding for the railways if they were to compete successfully with road transport and short haul air services. Yet against the odds in 1986, passenger services were resumed between Waverley and Bathgate, initially on an experimental basis. Several stations were re-opened in the Edinburgh area too, among them Livingston South, South Gyle and Wester Hailes, bringing more business to Waverley Station.

An additional 'state of the art' signalling centre was completed in 1986. With the railway going 'electronic', computerised ticket issuing and accounting systems had replaced the historic Edmonston method. A Solari train information board now 'flip-flopped' arrivals and departures. In 1987 'Second Class' became 'Standard Class' and the Sprinter era arrived with Class 150s. Greater attention was being paid to passenger access and a year later brick structures for lifts were built on some platforms when an old luggage bridge and hoists were removed.

From 1975, electrification of the East Coast main line had been proceeding. First proposed by the North Eastern Railway in 1920, this was to have a big impact on the 'look' of Waverley Station and its operation. The masts carrying wires from the West Coast route had reached the West End of Waverley by 1989 – without Bank of Scotland objections. Extra fencing was essential along Princes Street Gardens and this made 'train spotting' there virtually impossible. In 1991, the East Coast electrification was completed to Edinburgh and from then on, InterCity 225s would maintain the tradition of East Coast expresses in and out of Waverley. Soon the North Berwick branch was also 'under the wires'. Nevertheless, only the through platforms on the north and south flanks of the station's main 'island' were electrified at this time.

The Royal Scotsman, a luxury train touring the scenic routes of the Highlands began running in 1985. Today, it recalls the 'grand luxe' carriages of times past with its 'staterooms' for overnight accommodation. For other passengers, the withdrawal of sleeper services was a vexed question. Night travel by train was losing ground to faster day services, to airlines, and to motorway expresses. In 1988 when Euston became the sleeper terminus, the East Coast route was disadvantaged. The Caledonian Sleeper continues, the coaches being combined or split at Carstairs. It forms Britain's

The Solari information system advertised the Santa Specials in 1985. (Hamish Stevenson)

longest domestic train with Waverley contributing passengers to the Highland Sleeper portion.

On 1 April 1994, the process of consigning British Rail to history began. The 'privatisation' of the railways saw the disassembly of a highly integrated system that had evolved over decades. From now on, 'lines' would be divorced from the 'vehicles' that ran on them. Railtrack assumed responsibilities for track and infrastructure and some of Britain's major stations, including Waverley. Henceforth, leasing companies would provide rolling stock and an assortment of entrepreneurs would bid for 'franchises' – the right to provide services, closely specified for a fixed period of years. Accommodation had then to be found for their offices and staffs at Waverley.

In 1991 Waverley Station was 'A-listed' by Historic Scotland on account of its architectural and historic importance. Such listings are to safeguard Scotland's built heritage and promote its understanding and enjoyment. (A note states that the listing does not include internal additions or replacements made at the station in recent years).

Since 1992 any works undertaken at Waverley Station have therefore been subject to listed building consent requiring consultation with Historic Scotland. Between 1997 and 1999

Below left: By the 1980s, a solitary Class 8 locomotive sufficed for shunting duties at Waverley's east end. (J.L. Stevenson)
Below: In 1985 Class 37 022 in new livery passes Waverley West signal box with the Royal Scotsman train in its inaugural year. (Bruce Peter)

Railtrack's 'Station Regeneration Programme' brought repairs to the station, the roof and some redecoration. Traffic circulation from Waverley Bridge was re-organised with the north ramp closed to all but permitted vehicles while the south ramp was adapted to take two-way traffic. This enabled a pedestrian concourse, facing a new digital departure board, to be created in the core of the station. Flanked by two glass-fronted pavilions, it leads to gated access to the west platforms. However, the grand train shed is compromised by the assortment of retail stalls – and their lack of design coherence – that detract from this noble public space.

In 2003 an architectural competition for Waverley Station was again mooted, with all options open from restoration to demolition. Edinburgh City Council favoured the 'greening' of the valley west of Waverley Bridge by putting a grass roof over the station. A massive retail development, with a central atrium to admit some light, would then be placed on a deck above the railway lines – making Waverley into another Birmingham New Street.

However, by 2004 Network Rail had been established, wiser counsels prevailed and thankfully refurbishment was the way forward. Waverley Station is emerging 'as good as new' from a perceptive series of projects. With passenger numbers at an all time 'high', it is busier than ever and continues to fulfil its crucial role at the very heart of the city of Edinburgh.

Above: This view from Regent's Road in 1990 shows Waverley's Calton Road entrance with the abandoned Jeffrey Street footbridge (centre left) on the roof. (J.L. Stevenson)

Left: The name 'ScotRail' was coined in the 1980s – here Class 117 DMUs are seen 'nose to tail' at Waverley. (Author's Collection)

Below: A high speed train in GNER livery leaves a much cleaner Waverley in the 1990s – a car park has replaced the goods yard and the frontage is under repair. (C. Naples/Stevenson Collection)

Waverley Station is noted for the variety of locomotives and trains that may be seen there

Top left: An East Coast HST leaves Waverley for Kings Cross.

Top right: A ScotRail Class 158 DMU emerges from Calton Tunnel.

Centre: East Coast's re-launched 'Flying Scotsman' with a Class 91 prepares to head south while a Class 334 in SPT colours waits with a Milngavie service.

Lower left: A CrossCountry Voyager about to leave for Manchester.

Lower right: A Class 90 in First ScotRail livery for service on the Caledonian Sleeper.

Above: A First Group TransPennine Class 185 approaching Waverley.
Right: A Virgin Voyager Class 221 calls at Platform 11.
Below: The A1 4-6-2 No.60163 Tornado comes to Waverley in 2009.
(Bruce Peter)

Opposite top: A West Coast Railways' Class 47 on 'The Royal Scotsman' train.
Opposite bottom left: A ScotRail Class 380 prepares for a North Berwick service.
Opposite bottom right: A DB Schenker (ex-EWS) Class 90 for sleeper duties.

Top left: A Class 334 in ScotRail livery at Platform 8W with works ongoing there.
Top right: West Coast Railways' Class 37 locomotives on an excursion train.
Centre: Former Strathclyde Passenger Transport Class 334 units on the services to Edinburgh via Bathgate.
Left: A DB (ex-EWS) Class 67 locomotive on West Coast Railways' Mk.2 coaches for peak time Fife Circle trains.

The on-going refurbishment at Edinburgh Waverley in 2011

From left to right,
1. The Waverley Steps project beside the Balmoral Hotel.
2. The repair and glazing of the roof (the east section is well advanced in this view, with the former Jeffrey Street footbridge in encapsulation).
3. The twin North and South Ramps, part of the concourse and drainage works.
4. Market Street bridge, platforms and car park works.

The Refurbishment

As Waverley Station is Britain's second largest station after London's Waterloo, any comprehensive programme of work to improve its appearance, access and operation would be challenging. There were many interests to be considered – the planning authority, retail units and services, taxis, neighbouring hotels, disability groups and, not least, passengers. Network Rail Scotland has its own staff to run the station while British Transport Police are responsible for its security. Although ScotRail, currently operated by First Group, has the bulk of the services at the station, there are four other franchise holders – East Coast, TransPennine, Arriva CrossCountry and Virgin Trains. There are also special services, such as The Royal Scotsman, and excursions to be accommodated. Waverley is thus a busy place and the liveries of the trains make it more colourful than ever.

To assist the smooth and safe operation of Waverley, in 2006 signalling had been revamped in an 'Integrated Electronic Control Centre', designed by DeltaRail and housed in a new extension above the 1970s facility. The new system featured automatic route setting, enabling all routine signalling activities to run without intervention by the signaller. This left staff free to focus on 'the management of exceptions, incidents or problems' – of pivotal significance at Waverley where over 900 train movements take place each day.

From January 2006 extensive re-aligning of the tracks at the western approach to the station was undertaken. This improved the layout and augmented capacity across the width of the west throat. Platform lengthening, including the replacement of canopies on verandas, was also completed. The final stage involved raising masts for further electrification in advance of the opening of the Airdrie-Bathgate Rail Link in December 2010 that resulted in 24 more trains per day at Waverley.

Within the station, the very first escalator had been installed between the concourse and the mezzanine level in December 2006; consequently, a new footbridge had to

Left: The Signalling Centre, dating from 1976, was revamped for 'Integrated Electronic Control' in 2006. Here the manager reviews train movements.

Extensive track works and platform re-shaping were carried out at Waverley's west side from 2006:

Above: With the canopies renewed, track was replaced while platforms were rebuilt in January 2007. (John Peter)

Lower left: A steel bridge deck being installed at New Street, east of Waverley Station in October 2011. (Network Rail)

Lower right: With electrification completed, Waverley West has a different look.

A bridge extension at the mezzanine level involved a new structure to take passengers to and from the north side platforms and to provide access between the Waverley Steps and the main concourse. This work was completed in the summer of 2006. (Network Rail)

be built as a link between the mezzanine and this escalator. To add extra platforms for trains, space from former carriage sidings by the North Wall was transformed into Platform 1 on its west side and Platform 20 on its east. Track work was re-jigged with an adjacent scissors crossing, thus permitting flexibility in placing trains. A temporary footbridge was erected to allow access to the Princes Mall Shopping Centre when the Waverley Steps project would come on stream; it was removed in January 2012. In addition, a 'Platform 10' was made on the north side by the Klondyke Wall. Much of this work could only be done at night or during 'blockades' – days such as Christmas and New Year when no trains ran. Further improvements to track continued – in the autumn of 2011 timber decking on the girder bridge at New Street, carrying lines from the Calton Tunnel, was replaced with steel.

Network Rail Scotland, supported by Transport Scotland, has risen to the challenge of refurbishment. It has led a team of experienced and purposeful contractors to achieve a remarkable transformation at the station. Before refurbishment could commence, enabling works were carried out. These began as 'Pack 1' by May Gurney in September 2009. A key factor was ensuring sufficient space for site compounds in and around the station. The first area identified was the old 'GPO Compound' to the east of the main building. This was where mail was once handled at the principal Edinburgh sorting office and a double deck bridge ran to platforms 1 and 2. When vacated by the Post Office, the area was used for executive car parking and servicing by the Balmoral Hotel, plus some station parking. After scaffolding was erected the linking bridge was removed during engineering possessions. With the site cleared and fenced off, a large welfare compound was available that December.

Another essential requirement was an improved high voltage electrical power feed for the station and the Signalling Centre. This both reduced the risk of power failures and, should these occur, improve recovery times; the feeds were commissioned in the spring of 2010.

Waverley Station's first escalators were installed in 2006. (Network Rail)

Above: Prefabricated track work at Waverley's north platforms, with an essential scissors crossing having been put in place in December 2006. (Network Rail)
Left: The north side extension for platforms 1 and 20 under construction in order to increase the station's capacity. (Network Rail)
Below: The frame for a staircase giving access through the Klondyke Wall to a new Platform 10. (Network Rail)

Above: While the Waverley Steps project took place, a temporary bridge was required on the north side for accessing the Princes Mall Shopping Centre.

Above and left: Once the Steps project was complete, the temporary bridge was removed in January 2012 during a possession on the north lines when no trains ran.

The Waverley Steps

In popular culture, the Waverley Steps were probably the best known feature of Waverley Station. There were steps on the site from the 1800s as a steep bank rose between the Little Mound and Princes Street. In 1847 the opening of a station at Canal Street, well below the level of Princes Street, necessitated twin flights of steps from its platforms to reach that thoroughfare. When the North British Railway acquired the site in 1865, stone steps were formed further east to access the company's station.

For years, passengers faced struggling up the Waverley Steps with luggage and prams while trying to dodge those people bounding downwards to catch trains. The Steps were steep, a '72 step nightmare', and impossible for the infirm or wheelchair users. Furthermore, they seemed to create their own weather. Blasts of air – a wind tunnel effect – caused discomfort and occasionally embarrassment. The Waverley Steps were the butt of Music Hall jokes – a breezy chasm where hats blew off and clothing was disarrayed by unpredictable gusts.

Escalator replacements for the Steps were discussed as long ago as 1923 but apart from a modest refurbishment in 1998, the Steps remained largely unchanged. There were seven flights used by an estimated 14,000 passengers each day – in fact, over a third of all passengers at Waverley Station tackled them. In 2004 Network Rail decided to include the Steps redevelopment as part of a major overhaul for Waverley Station. Soon proposals were on paper to install escalators and lifts but these met with some opposition from adjacent proprietors. Meanwhile, consultations showed that there was overwhelming public support for escalators.

To carry out improvements, Network Rail applied for a 'Waverley Steps Order' under the Transport and Works (Scotland) Act 2007. This 'TAWS' order, obtained in May 2010, conferred wide-ranging powers, including compulsory purchase and access for maintenance. Edinburgh City Council gave listed building consent. The £7 million enhancement – in tune with policies aimed at improving stations, augmenting capacity and enhancing passenger experience, while encouraging a modal shift to rail – was funded by Transport Scotland.

Waverley Station, being 'low set', has long presented problems of access for passengers – there were five different points, all with deficiencies concerning disability compliance. The Disability Discrimination Act 1995 (DDA) required the rail industry to assist disabled people in accessing stations wherever possible. Accordingly, escalators and lifts would allow the mobility impaired to reach all platforms at Waverley. 'The Steps Project' should provide weather protected, properly lit, step-free access at last.

Various options for the difficult site were considered. The choice settled on three banks of twin escalators linking to the station's internal mezzanine bridge and connecting to all platforms. In addition, there would be eight new flights of steps with a sandstone finish; a glazed canopy of modern design, supported by tree-like pillars, would be a permanent 'umbrella'. Adjacent to the Princes Mall Shopping Centre, a raised walkway at roof level would lead to two lifts accessing the mezzanine level. These were more contentious as an Act of 1872 for the North British Railway prohibited certain structures from being more than 12.8m (42ft) above rail height and prevented any new building within the station footprint from rising above 14.8m (48.5ft) from the tracks. However, this restriction had to be relaxed to permit the lift shafts to be 25.1m (82.3ft) above rail level.

The architects for the Steps Project and other elements in the refurbishment were Jefferson Sheard. As Waverley Station is 'A listed' by Historic Scotland and the Balmoral Hotel is 'B listed', the designs had to be sensitive to both and to the surrounding city area, part of a World Heritage Site. The Steps Project would give the station a modern 'front door' on Princes Street – an entrance that it has long lacked.

Despite its railway origins, the luxury Balmoral Hotel, owned by the Forte Group, feared loss of business through having a building site adjacent. Exception was taken to the proposed lift shafts interrupting views to Edinburgh Castle from a popular function suite. A public local inquiry was held in July 2009 and only on the last day were the hotel group's objections withdrawn. The lifts had to be re-sited. A Code of Construction Practice was drawn up restricting hours of work while dust, noise and vibration levels would have to be carefully controlled to limit disturbance and air pollution. With the Steps site being so small, it would prove operationally fraught – 'like trying to decorate the living room through the letterbox on the front door'.

Morgan Sindall plc were the contractors for 'The Steps Project' and set up base on the roof of the Princes Shopping Mall. The team faced a ravine under slope with a rise of 12m (36ft). When work began on removing the old steps, access for hotel staff and fire exits had to be maintained. So tight was the Steps site that mini-machines, materials and spoil had to be lifted in and out by crawler-cranes. Scaffolding had to be erected, taken down and put up again as the tempo of construction varied on site.

The escalators came from Kone, a leading Finnish company, with the first being installed on 28 August 2011. These had been assembled at the Kone factory in Yorkshire and bringing the escalators to Princes Street involved complex negotiations with Police, Lothian Transport, and the Balmoral Hotel. Part of Princes Street was closed to accommodate a 500 tonne crane. (Although each escalator weighed just 8 tonnes, lifting from street level down to the lower steps was a reach of 65m, hence the need for a big crane with a long jib). Soon the first pair of escalators was coaxed into position – a landmark for 'The Steps Project' – then sheeted up for protection while work went ahead on the staircases and canopy. The second batch for the upper

sections was placed on 16 October, ahead of schedule, on a calm, warm day.

The framework for the canopy was stainless steel designed to hold heavy glazing panels. Preparing foundations for the canopy's tapering columns meant piling in most restrictive conditions. Another troublesome process was the removal of a masonry arch at the foot of the Steps and its replacement with a steel beam integral with the station roof. The canopy's assembly, welding, machining and fixing took many hours, the team working day and night to complete it. Glazing followed but fitting seals to keep out moisture between the thick glass panels was time consuming. Meanwhile, wood effect panelling was fixed to the west sidewall and soon lighting and CCTV equipment was installed. Finally, the new stairs were faced with sandstone, masonry was restored, shop fronts painted and balustrades set in place. After much testing, the escalators were declared ready for public use.

Attention could then be given to forming ramps for disabled access over the Shopping Mall's roof and to installing lifts to the footbridge above platform 20. The area for the ramps was excavated and waterproofed prior to being clad in grey granite. Flowerbeds, using lightweight compost, were incorporated in the design and the main passageway to the lifts was floored with sandstone slabs.

In August 2011 the first escalators required a 500 tonne crane to be on site.

Stannahs supplied the lifts at both the Market Street and the Steps' sites. Bespoke lifts of large sizes have become a speciality – the two glass-fronted lifts at the Steps can each accommodate 16 people. Preparatory to their installation, considerable construction and electrical work was done on the platform beneath. The lifts have become a surprise attraction giving a panoramic view over Waverley's roof from the North Bridge and the spires of the Old Town to Edinburgh Castle.

On 14 August 2012 David Simpson, Route Managing Director Network Rail Scotland, welcomed Keith Brown, MSP, Minister for Transport in the Scottish Government, to the official opening of the Steps Project.

Right: The narrow site between a luxury hotel and a shopping mall was challenging.
Below: All supplies had to be lifted in and spoil or waste lifted out.
Opposite: Removal of the old steps in progress with an access maintained for hotel staff.

Above: A mini excavator at work at the Steps site.
Top right: Bricking up the Shopping Centre wall.
Right: With a task completed, the mini-excavator is prepared for lifting out.
Below: Throughout all the Waverley projects, 'reduce, reuse and recycle' was the aim.

Waverley Steps Waste Reduction

So far we have recycled:

82.2% of our Construction waste

100% of our Demolition waste

100% of our Excavation waste

REDUCE ➡ REUSE ➡ RECYCLE

Top left: A piling rig in action on the difficult site.
Top right: A formwork for new steps being put in place.
Above: The route map for bringing large cranes into Central Edinburgh.
Right: Preparing the base for an escalator.

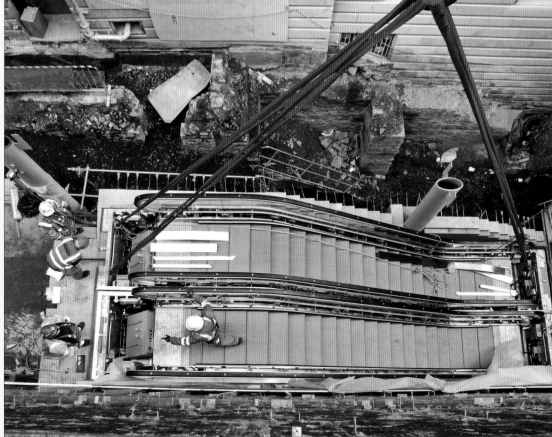

Opposite: Looking towards the old station with the entrance construction site in full swing.
Above: Into the chasm goes the first escalator early on 28 August 2011.
Right: The second one is eased into position.

Top left: Once in place, the first escalators were sheeted up as work continued around them.

Top right: The second batch arrived on 16 October 2011, stopping traffic in Princes Street.

Above: Another big crane begins the lift of an escalator.

Above: Coaxing an escalator into line.
Below: An escalator is slowly swung into place on its concrete foundation.
Right: Gently does it as an escalator touches base.

Top left and right: Checking the position of the escalators before final adjustments are made.
Below: End of the day and there's satisfaction with a job well done.

Top left: A view from above of the awkward location where an entrance with a masonry arch met the station roof.

Top right: The new wider entrance to the station takes shape.

Left: With old masonry removed, work pressed on to form the new entrance.

Above: Engineers and scaffolders contemplate the narrow work site.

Above and above right: Assembling the steelwork for the new canopy.
Right: The design element where the branches of the support columns meet the glazing.
Below: Installing the glazing on the canopy structure.

Top left: Building scaffolding for the lift works adjacent to the Shopping Mall roof.
Top right: The scaffold in debris netting with the new canopy at the Steps' site on the right.
Middle left: Work advancing on the lifts at the station's mezzanine level.
Middle right: A lift shaft is built up piece by piece.
Left: The support structure for the lifts on Platform 20.

Top left: The lift entrances on the Shopping Mall roof.

Top right: The lifts nearing completion at the mezzanine level.

Centre: Laying slabs on the Shopping Mall roof.

Lower left: Concrete walls for the ramp access on the roof.

Lower middle: Granite steps were built on the roof giving access to Princes Street.

Lower right: As granite edging was installed, a planting scheme was completed.

Left: By night the tree design of the canopy becomes apparent. (John Peter)
Below: Finishing touches at the Princes Street entrance to the new escalators.
Bottom: The escalators in action with passenger usage now higher than forecast.

The Train Shed Roof

At Waverley Station, the roof is the key defining element, both externally and internally – hence its glazing with clear glass would be transformational, filling the station with light.

The principal contractor for this package was Balfour Beatty plc one of the leading firms in the civil engineering and construction industry. The scope of the works was so extensive that extra compounds were required. A strategic yard was arranged at Calton Road, and in addition to providing secure site access, it housed shot blast pots, extraction systems for paint debris, storage for glass and other facilities. For the east roof, there was a scaffolding staircase for the workforce and a hoist to take supplies up to roof level and allow the removal of scrap. The aim was to recycle as much material – existing glazing, old wood and metal – achieving a target of 93 per cent.

The roof 'package' covered the refurbishment, repair and painting of all steelwork including the supporting columns. The current roof, dating from 1898, had left an immense steel frame where over 27,400 panels of new glass would be installed in an area equivalent to 14 football pitches (34,000m²). A new roof drainage system with syphonic outlets was designed; the down pipes within the tall support columns were abandoned – the outlets being either blocked or corroded. However, the cast iron and steel roof gutters were re-proofed and re-used. On the east roof, a unique feature that was retained in part was the Jeffrey Street footbridge. Although closed since 1958, this retention, requested by Edinburgh City Council and Historic Scotland, resulted in the re-cladding of its roof. On the west side, the former North British link from the station to the Balmoral Hotel was renovated and also re-roofed. However, other disused bridges from the main station building were removed.

A work site was created high above the station's platforms and tracks. Complex scaffolding, demanding innovative solutions for its support, was erected from east to west across the entire station area as work progressed. Some scaffolding was attached to existing structures such as the Klondyke Wall or other masonry supports. Towers were also constructed from the station floor around the tall roof columns. Lightweight aluminium bridge panels on thick steel wires were held in suspension from the station roof itself – notably around the main building, the concourse and platform areas. At one stage, 60 per cent of the glazed station area was beneath scaffolding; nevertheless, there were space restrictions for scaffolds as the safe movement of people was of paramount importance.

The working deck of profiled steel sheeting allowed both for constructional activity on the roof and supported additional lightweight scaffolding right up to ridge height. The deck had also to protect the public and station staff from falling objects and from rain when glazing was removed. It was floored with plywood as a safeguard against dropped tools and was then covered with a double layer of

Job done – the transverse 'ridge and furrows' of the re-glazed west roof of Waverley Station. (John Peter)

synthetic membranes to give environmental protection and reduce dust and noise levels. It was gently sloped to carry rainwater away to channels and temporary gullies for drainage. For many months and six days a week, teams of men worked overhead while passengers using the station were unaware of their presence. Much scaffolding was done on night shifts.

Tackling the roof involved stripping back steel and cast iron by shot blasting before specialist coatings could be applied. Health and environmental protection issues were priorities. So work locations were 'encapsulated' to prevent dust or contaminants, such as lead particles, reaching the environment. This was done with 'Envirowrap', a flameproof plastic sheeting which had been proven on the Forth Bridge. The metalwork was shot blasted with abrasive grit piped by compressed air from up to 600m away, while at ground level, shot blast 'pots' were replenished by technicians. The debris was sucked away by industrial cleaning equipment prior to careful disposal in special facilities off site.

Once bare metal was exposed, it gave the best possible surface for the application of new paint but this had to be done immediately before deterioration began. Experience gained on the Forth Bridge resulted in a 'three coat' method being used. First came spray painting with a primer followed by a stripe coat applied by brush. The topcoat chosen was 'ash white'. Finally, any points where scaffolding had been attached were covered. The tall columns with Corinthian capitals, supporting the station roof, had special treatment being painted in green, cream and gold.

The glazing selected was laminated glass giving noise reduction and thermal insulation. In addition to being energy efficient, it gives a durable cover protecting from impact. Secured in a 'bespoke patent glazing system', there is air space between the panes for ventilation. For safe access to maintain and repair the roof, fixed walkways and moveable gantries were devised – essential as the Waverley roof is the third largest glazed structure in the United Kingdom. The first pane was installed on 21 April 2011, an event overseen by Ron McAulay, then Director of Network Rail Scotland.

An episode that put the working deck and station operations at risk occurred early on 17 May 2012. A 12in Scottish Water mains pipe on the underside of the North Bridge

The flood, from a burst water main, descends into the north concourse in May 2012. (Network Rail)

burst. The water poured down onto the new roof filling up the principal gutter in the area. This then overflowed onto the suspended working deck. As the deluge continued for several hours, the deck itself was soon under 6in of water – and it was not designed to take such an extra load – so all workmen present were summoned to punch holes in the deck to allow the water to escape down into the station and relieve the weight.

The station's refurbishment faced several issues one of which was trespassers attempting to enter the work sites or to find a sheltered spot to spend the night. At the North Bridge, sections of the main roof have been reinforced and steel clad to prevent persons falling into the station and posing an ongoing risk to staff and station users.

The mock-up of a portion of the roof in the main yard of Balfour Beatty.

Top left: The lattice girder supporting the station roof by the Calton Road site entrance.
Top right: The scaffolding staircase for roof access at Calton Road.
Centre left: The controlled entry to the restricted Calton Road site.
Centre middle: A crane lifts materials for roof repairs.
Centre right: The hoist that took supplies up and brought waste down for re-cycling.
Lower left: As the workshop floor spread, day became night at the Balfour Beatty complex on the east concourse.
Lower right: Welfare facilities were available round the clock at the site.

Above top left and right: The east roof looking towards Calton Hill, and the west roof looking towards the Scott Monument, showing their unsatisfactory condition.

Centre left: On the workshop floor, the overhead electrification had to be respected.

Centre right: Lightweight scaffolding was erected on the workshop floor. (Network Rail)

Lower left: Up close, the roof was in need of attention as this defective plastic shows.

Lower right: The sorry state of the capitals on the roof's support columns; these contained down pipes for drainage. (Network Rail)

Top left: A technician supplying the grit for blasting.
Top centre: A stockpile of grit at the Calton Road site.
Top right: Spent grit was sucked up by industrial cleaning equipment for disposal at special sites.
Centre: Blasters in action in the confined spaces high in Waverley's roof. (Network Rail)
Left: Air was extracted and filtered from the encapsulated areas during shot blasting.

Top: With the steel stripped to bare metal, painters immediately set to work. Here final 'touching up' is being done. From the roof structure, suspension wires supported the workshop floor. (Network Rail)

Above: An awkward location where the roof structure met masonry by Calton Road.

Centre right: Light weight scaffolding enabled all parts of the roof to be reached. Here Senior Project Engineer Alastair Barclay inspects progress.

Right: To protect new paint, polystyrene sleeves were used, here emphasising the scale of the roof structure.

Top left: Shifting scaffolding from a newly completed section on the east roof – a routine task.

Top right: The roof has awkward angles and features such as the cupola above the booking hall, here carefully protected.

Centre: A paint tin crusher reduced waste going off site.

Lower left and right: Painters at work on the west roof adjacent to the Balmoral Hotel.

Top left: Moving glazing panels in the Calton Road yard.
Top right: Preparing to install glazing on the east roof.
Right: Steel being repaired on the east roof.
Lower left: With a gutter re-proofed, a gantry for safe access is constructed on the east roof.
Lower right: On the west roof, a trolley comes along with more glazing panels.

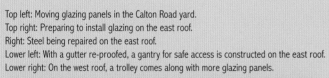

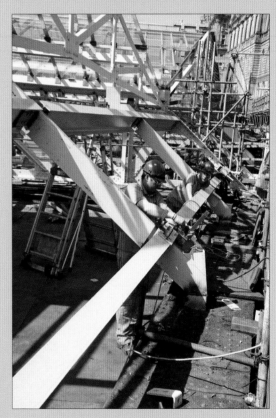

Top left: Making up brackets for the glazing system.
Top right: Measuring up for the glazing on the west roof.
Centre: All kitted up — but it's a hot day on the roof.
Lower left: Using the gutter lines for access, the glazing is carefully placed.
Lower right: The glazing panel is then secured.

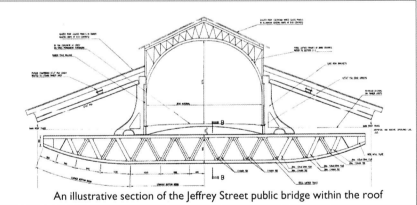

An illustrative section of the Jeffrey Street public bridge within the roof

Above: The framework for the Jeffrey Street footbridge, an old link from Calton Road at roof height across the station.

Lower left: Completing scaffolding for the partial restoration involving only the roof structure.

Lower right: Waverley's east roof, seen from the north side, with the footbridge area under encapsulation.

Top left and right: The steel structure of the footbridge when painting was ongoing.
Left: Nearing completion; the planks would later be removed. (Network Rail)
Lower right: Wrapped in plastic sheeting, the footbridge had been hidden from view.
Lower left: The final result from within the station shows only the footbridge roof above.

Inspecting a new drain access point on the east concourse.

During refurbishment, the columns were encased in scaffolding. The latter's footprint was restricted in order to maximise circulation areas for staff and public.

The columns, which no longer function as down pipes, have had their capitals restored and painted in gold.

Excavations as much as 7.5m down were dug out.

Improved drainage linked to existing major sewers was constructed beneath the station.

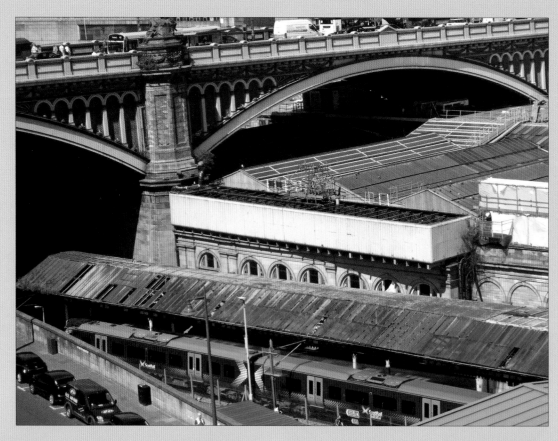

Top: By a pier of the North Bridge, this large cistern or water tank once supplied the station and engines with water.
Centre left: Demolishing the cast iron panels of the tank. (Network Rail)
Centre right: The supporting portion of the Klondyke Wall beneath the tank.
Lower left: While trains ran, the tank was taken apart — a view from the North Bridge.
Lower right: A sandstone parapet was built where the tank once stood on top of the Klondyke Wall.

Concourse and Ramps

All platform surfaces under the train shed (though omitting platforms 1, 10 and 20) have been renewed right out to the eastern extremities. At the same time, the opportunity has been taken to improve platform drainage that previously ran off to track sides. An activity of which passengers become very aware was the laying of a new sandstone concourse with granite edging to replace the previous tiling. This caused portions of the circulation areas to be fenced off in rotation as the programme advanced, but access to and from platforms had to be kept while trains were running.

The City of Edinburgh Council had concerns about possible closure of the north and south ramps, the main arteries leading into the station, when waterproofing and resurfacing were undertaken. In May 2011 the south ramp was tackled when a temporary taxi rank was placed on Market Street; meanwhile, arrangements had to be made at New Street car park and also with East Coast to assist passengers with mobility problems.

Beneath the station concourse, there was a deep drainage system that tied into pipes leading to the city's Nor Loch sewer – the origins of which go back to the latter's removal in the 1760s. From both east and west concourses, access shafts were opened as much as 7.5m down to tap old conduits. When the south ramp was closed, the opportunity was grasped of carrying out deep drainage works there. Debris was cleared out, new pipes were inserted and concrete poured to improve structures with much work being done at night to minimise station disruption and noise. All the south road area was then re-surfaced.

Subsequently the steelwork beneath both ramps was repaired and painted. The old cast iron balustrades were reinstated throughout, with original examples being used to make moulds for the purpose by Ballantines of Bo'ness.

The cleaning and repair of defective masonry saw much work carried out both on the North Wall and the Klondyke Wall. On the latter, a large redundant water tank by the North Bridge was carefully removed to prevent damage to the wall. With its cast iron panels taken apart, a crane positioned at night on the North Bridge hauled them up for disposal. Masons then built a new sandstone cornice and parapet on the Klondyke Wall to keep the original profile.

A team of scaffolders prepares for a night shift above the concourse.

Waverley by night: Under floodlights work continued with the great station empty of passengers and staff.

An elevating platform with scaffolding in suspension above the concourse.

The Calton Road yard kept up grit supply for shotblasting at all hours.

A scaffolding store in a yard by Platform 11.

Above: Action on the concourse by night where some scaffolding is being taken down and surface works continue.
Right: Preparations for re-surfacing the concourse on the east side at night.
Below: A view of the deserted station – an engineering possession, plus the isolation of electrical installations, enables the workshop floor to advance above the north platforms.

Historic elements on the concourse date from the 1890s reconstruction.

Top left: The handsome east façade of the main building.

Top right: The initials of the North British Railway on a frieze.

Centre: With ornamental wrought iron banisters, these station stairs lead to Calton Road.

Lower left: The north ramp prior to its repair showing the 'drip trays' inserted latterly to catch drainage.

Lower right: The way it was – Stuart's Granolithic Stone Company of Edinburgh were surfacing specialists in the 1890s when the station was rebuilt.

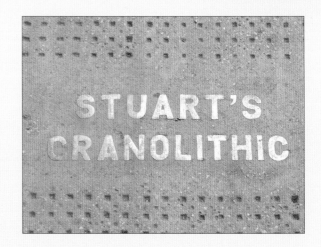

Top left: Twin columns supporting the mezzanine footbridge on the main concourse show an amalgam of classical idioms.
Top right: The distinctive mezzanine footbridge above the main concourse acts as a spine across the station.
Middle right: The cast iron balustrade in neo-classical style when under repair on the station ramps.
Lower left and right: A sandstone wall by the south ramp shows classical detailing in its columns and corner baluster.

While refurbishment progressed, normal station functions had to continue.

Above top to bottom:
The ScotRail Ticket Office.
Left luggage facilities.
A curious 1980s addition to station offices.

Above top to bottom:
The ScotRail First Class Lounge.
Ticket machines in the main booking hall.
The well used cycle racks.

Top and centre: With work ongoing on the train shed roof above, 2km of platform repairs and improvements were also under way as here at platform 4. (Network Rail)
Lower: On the concourse, the old surface was excavated prior to the new base being laid while preserving ducts for utilities.

Top left: For access by occasional buses, heavy duty granite slabs, in keeping with the station's character, were placed on part of the main concourse.
Top right: As the concourse was grubbed up in stages, sound blankets were used to reduce noise.
Centre right: A Rail Gourmet trolley crosses the expanse of newly laid east concourse.
Lower left: The bulk of the concourse was re-surfaced with specially prepared sandstone slabs.
Lower right: Safe access to trains and to retail premises had to be maintained during this phase.

Top: The main concourse under wraps as the workshop floor advances in suspenion overhead.
Centre right: Retail units hidden in encapsulation on the main concourse.
Lower left: The tall cast iron columns, concealed in scaffolding, were sealed off.
Lower right: 'How do I get to the platform?' Open mesh panels kept the information boards visible.

Top: Keeping the public informed required altering signage and train information.
Centre: The retail stalls below the mezzanine bridge on the main concourse had to be shifted around as the re-surfacing advanced.
Lower left and right: Notwithstanding the on-going work, retail outlets managed to keep in business 'as usual'.

Top left: For access to the main cab stand, priority repairs were carried out on the south ramp at an early stage.

Top right: The taxi rank at Waverley with the workshop deck above.

Centre left: During work on ramps, two banksmen were on duty for all deliveries to ensure safety.

Centre right, lower left and right: Shifting waste, bringing in supplies and removing equipment after use were problems encountered daily.

Above: Temporary use had to be made of the north ramp for taxis while the south access was closed.

Right: Asphalt being spread for the passenger access on the north ramp. Note the heritage lamp standard has been restored.

Below: 'No admittance' — guarding the entrance to the north ramp while concrete for kerbing was being poured.

Market Street

Waverley's Market Street entry on the south side was dingy, inadequate and outmoded. The platforms and verandas, relics of the 'South Sub', were decaying. A complete reconstruction was therefore planned involving a new glazed and spacious footbridge connecting with the station's mezzanine level, plus new staircases and lifts both to platforms and to the New Street car park. The plan foresaw the replacement of the decrepit canopies over platforms 8 and 9 with modern glazed installations for which the cast iron supports would be re-used. In addition to the platforms, the New Street car park would be re-surfaced. These major upgrades were entrusted to C Spencer Ltd.

The Market Street work site was awkward – being long, dark and narrow, tucked under premises where sidings had once existed. Platforms 8 and 9 are on an island with restricted space on which to set up site compounds. In addition, C Spencer also faced time limitations driven by the need to ensure that full scheduled train services would be maintained during the project.

Under package 3 the works began in June 2011. Principally, these would deliver a new bridge at the Market Street entrance giving step free access into Waverley Station, plus stairs and lifts to platforms 8 and 9. 'Gull wing' canopies of contemporary design above modern staircases would complement those placed on the platform verandas.

Two key factors impacted on this complex package of works – the necessity to maintain access through the south side of Waverley Station when the old footbridge was taken away and the new one built, and how to bring materials and machines to the site compound. This would be via New Street car park that had only a maximum headroom of 2 metres – hopeless for big cranes. To overcome this problem, the C Spencer team obtained permission from Edinburgh City Council Highways Department to construct a substantial temporary ramp from East Market Street into the car park.

First, a temporary bridge structure had to be designed to cross from Market Street to the station. C Spencer worked with their scaffolding contractor to find a means to span the tracks safely in the minimum time. The technique was to build scaffold bridge decks above but adjacent to the tracks at platforms 8 and 9 and then to 'launch' them across the gap on runners. After assembly in a yard by Platform 9, the south span was launched across the track and secured on a structure on the island platform. The north span over Platform 8 to the Klondyke Wall was then propelled out in 'piggy back' style to fill the gap.

Within the station there was a similar launch to create a long scaffold span from platform 11 to the Klondyke Wall. With the spans meeting at that point, a hole of suitable size had to be made in the wall. As the masonry was removed – in blocks weighing up to 500kg – each piece was numbered for reinstatement. An elaborate scaffolding was then built for a temporary bridge to go through the wall and be long enough to reach ground at platform 11. The facing parapet in Market Street had also to be breached.

With the temporary bridge structure in position, it was waterproofed, lined, painted and fitted out with lighting and signage. Remembered as a labyrinth, it contained a corridor and stairs for safe passage for the daily procession of passengers, plus lift and stair access for platforms 8 and 9 and to New Street car park. There was also a hoist to allow Rail Gourmet to service trains.

Soon a crane was lifting out the old timber footbridge bit by bit. When the canopies were stripped off the platforms, the ironwork was shot blasted, and painting could begin. Meantime, the work site was tight and like the Steps project, 'crane dependent'. Nevertheless, with piling done and steelwork raised to support the new Market Street footbridge, construction forged ahead.

Once the steel canopies and staircases had been fabricated in the C Spencer yard, they were ready for installation. Using weekend 'possessions' with no trains on the tracks and the overhead line equipment (OLE) switched off, a succession of cranes lifted the parts into place. Additionally, there was brickwork to build, concrete to pour and tiling to be done. Masonry at the Market Street 'gate'

The cast iron supports and brackets for the canopies at platform 8 and 9 at Market Street.

The decrepit canopies at Market Street with the big water tank adjacent.

had to be repaired, handrails installed, and – not least – the glazed roof and wall panels for the new footbridge secured. The target for completion was the Edinburgh International Festival of 2012 when the remodelled Market Street entrance, now suffused with light, came into use.

The complex scaffolding could then be taken down. However, work continued on the platform canopies with extra strengthening being placed under the North Bridge. A west side staircase to platforms 8 and 9 with another 'gull wing' was also made.

A key section to be removed was known as the 'pod' – a structure adjacent to the Klondyke Wall, with stairs on the *south* side of the wall but leading to Platform 10 on the *north* side through an opening in the wall. Track possessions limited possibilities for the 'pod' removal to a station closure of 54 hours at Christmas 2012. So on Christmas Day, foregoing the festivities, the C Spencer team successfully cut and craned out the old section. In a slick operation with two cranes, they installed a new enclosed deck to allow passengers on and off Platform 10 for train services starting on 27 December.

During the refurbishment packages, extra works were identified. Attention turned to the Waverley Bridge where shot blasting, repair and painting of steelwork on its underside, plus east and west faces, was clearly desirable. Its support columns were similarly treated. With water seepage from the bridge an on-going problem, this would be corrected, giving protection to passengers on the west end platforms.

Further Work

For 'package 4', concerning the main station building, the principal contractor will again be C. Spencer. The priority is to make the fabric wind and watertight, beginning with resealing the roof and repairing or replacing the windows. High on the roof, any redundant air conditioning plant has already been removed. The decorative cupola above the main ticket hall will also have attention while the external walls will be cleaned. When the ticket hall floor has been re-surfaced, the interior will be refreshed with cleaning and painting.

Below ground, the main station boiler for the heating system is to be replaced with an energy efficient one and electrical installations rewired, including leads to retail outlets. What passengers will notice most will be new lifts to give step free access to the main building and to the ScotRail Operations Centre. An old lift shaft that once conveyed people to the North British Station Hotel (now the Balmoral) will be utilised. In the main ticket hall, scaffolding design will be crucial – it is a very busy place where the maximum area for people and luggage is essential but it is also over a basement restricting the load that the floor can take. These works are scheduled for completion by the end of 2013 by which time a vehicle security protection system, making for a safer station, will feature on the ramps.

The dingy approach to platforms 8 and 9 once used by the South Suburban trains.

Above: A view from the Scotsman Steps across the old Market Street entrance with the west roof of Waverley Station beyond.
Left: The old staircase from Market Street.
Below: The roofless structure on the west facing platforms at Market Street- hardly a welcoming place for passengers.

Top: The temporary ramp for access to the C. Spencer site at Market Street.
Centre left and left: The long narrow work site below the 'undercroft' where sidings once lay.
Above: 'Who's on a tea break?' Members of the Spencer team outside their site office at Market Street.

Top left: The temporary bridge allowing access between the main station and Market Street.

Top right: Watching the Market Street footbridge being cut away.

Above: A crane waits to lift out sections of the footbridge.

Centre right: A section on its way to re-cycling.

Right: The old Market Street entrance left 'high and dry'.

Top left: A hole had to be cut in the Klondyke Wall to permit temporary access arrangements between Market Street and the main station.
Top right: A view along platforms 7 and 11 showing the Klondyke Wall in scaffolding pending repairs – a responsibility of Balfour Beatty.
Centre left: Masons at work on the Klondyke Wall.
Centre right: Stones were carefully numbered and stored for replacement.
Lower left: What passengers saw of the temporary bridge from the concourse.
Lower right: The hole in the Klondyke Wall that allowed the temporary footbridge to go through.

Top left: Much work at Market Street was done under possessions when no trains ran on the tracks.

Top right: Cutting parts of the old canopy framework away to prepare room for the new.

Centre left: Scaffolders making preparations for the temporary bridge installation at Market Street.

Centre right: Ground under the platforms caused piling problems.

Lower left and right: Much work was done at night – here a crane hoists a new lift shaft into position.

Top left: With the canopy brackets conserved and shot blasted, it was time for an undercoat.
Top right: Encapsulation protected paintwork (and the painters) from the weather.
Centre left: The 'gull's wing' design of the new canopies above the staircases at Market Street.
Centre right upper: Assembling steelwork in the yard at Market Street.
Centre right lower: The C. Spencer site was crane dependent for the assembly of large components.
Left: For shot blasting, the encapsulation with 'Envirowrap' stretched east under and beyond the North Bridge.

Top: The frame for the new Market Street footbridge takes shape beside the temporary structure.
Centre: Masons at work hidden behind the debris netting.
Lower left: Delivery of canopy components was by road from Wishaw.
Lower right: A section of new canopy is lifted into position.

Top left: Brickwork going up for car park access.
Top right: A concrete delivery made possible by the temporary ramp from Market Street.
Centre left: Checking the piled supports for the new entrance at Market Street.
Centre right: The design is revealed as the stair canopies are formed.
Lower left: With the roof secured, activity moved indoors to a blue phase with much debris netting.
Lower right: Installing the handrails for a staircase.

Top left: Tiling in progress at the new Market Street entrance.
Top right: Masons repairing the stonework at the old entrance.
Left: An engineer checking levels with GPS equipment while stairways take shape.
Below: Sorting out a problem beside a new lift.

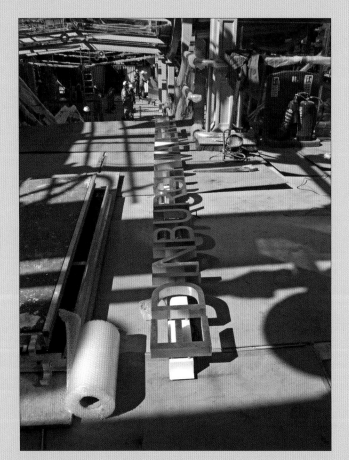

Top left: The dazzling prospect at the Market Street entrance once the netting was removed.
Top right: Checking seals on the glazing panels.
Lower left: The new name sign for 'Edinburgh Waverley' at Market Street.
Lower right: Finishing touches being applied in advance of the opening of the Market Street access to the public.

Top: Opening Day at the new Market Street entrance on 14 August 2012. (Project Manager Alastair Barclay is third from right in the foreground).
Centre and bottom: By day or night, the Market Street entrance is now an accessible and welcoming place for passengers.

Waverley People

While the refurbishment programme rolled out, the regular tasks for station staff had to continue – checking and selling tickets, servicing and despatching trains and assisting passengers with enquiries. Helping people find their way around a station that takes some knowing, became more important than ever as routes in and out varied. Meanwhile, the routine of the whole establishment had to be co-ordinated and that fell to Network Rail's Station Manager in overall charge with twenty-five Network Rail personnel on a shift system round the clock. 'Project Working Group' meetings and walkabouts to view progress claimed much management time.

At Waverley, as with other major stations in Britain, there is 'unimaginable complexity' compared with the years when a single over-arching organisation, such as the North British Railway, the LNER or its successor British Rail, held sway. Regular scheduled meetings of the various 'stakeholders' are the 'glue' that holds the different interests together and increasingly 'alliancing' between the parties is seen as the way forward.

"Where's Princes Street?" . . . "It's up there"

ScotRail, with the preponderance of trains, has the largest staff with over a hundred on its payroll. An unusual responsibility for ScotRail is the shunting of the Caledonian Sleeper in the middle of the night. It also has a 'signing on' point for train crews whose main base is an Operations Centre shared with other franchisees. For East Coast, staff numbers are 95, CrossCountry has 12, TransPennine 7, and Virgin has a similar number. All have had to be found offices in the station.

Supporting these businesses, there are ancillary teams – for example, Rail Gourmet supplies East Coast with food and drink from its depot in the station, and Initial Services' employees keep the station clean and free from litter.

British Transport Police are continually on patrol. Together with extra security personnel, they are a visible presence when the station is packed with sports fans going to a match, or platforms are thronged with enthusiasts eager to see a steam special.

The Station Manager has a full diary with station operations, station security and station access meetings in which franchise holders, stakeholders, tenants, retailers and the British Transport Police participate. Department of Transport security inspectors may also attend. In addition, there is special event planning, some of which involves liaison with the City of Edinburgh Council for the Festival Fireworks, marathons and fun runs, marches and rallies. Station control systems – whereby information is transferred to shift managers for display on boards or for public announcements – are regularly reviewed. Only on Christmas Day and Boxing Day is there an interlude – the station is closed to the public and no trains run. That is when the engineers can take over with a blockade on the lines.

As the refurbishment 'packages' progressed, Waverley's character changed temporarily – walls bristled with scaffolding, blue debris netting spread, and mysterious structures were hidden in plastic sheeting. Daylight disappeared as the steel deck advanced, and the artificially lit station took on a night ambience. Men in orange overalls and safety helmets went about their work; there was the roar of shot blasting, the smell of paint, of asphalt and of fresh concrete. But when the 'packages' were complete, light came flooding back into the station. With new escalators and lifts in place, Waverley was more user friendly than ever before and the inconveniences of timely refurbishment were soon forgotten. A balance had been struck between preserving the station's heritage and creating an environment that tries to meet the needs of passengers in the 21st century.

These improvements at Waverley Station would not be the conclusion of investment there by Network Rail Scotland. It was also announced that additional lifts on platforms and at Calton Road would further improve accessibility in projects continuing well into 2014.

Another light to be fixed.

Removing cabling at Market Street.

'Is this information correct?'

With a pedestrian access on the right, keeping the site at Market Street safe and clean was essential.

Paperwork gets attention.

A seat at the end of a shift.

Keeping hoardings secure.

Emergency repairs on the concourse.

Top left: Painting temporary structures.
Top right: The Project Management team on an inspection.
Lower: Scaffolders on the job.

Routine tasks continued throughout the refurbishment
Top left: Keeping the dust at bay.
Top centre: Coping with litter.
Top right: Cleaning coaches.
Below: Re-stocking train catering using a temporary hoist at Market Street.

ScotRail staff at the ticket gates. Every effort was made to keep the passenger experience positive.

Despatching trains on time.

Watering the toilets in coaches.

An old Police lamp from gas light days.

British Transport Police on the concourse on a quiet day.

The new lighting harmonises with the old station.

"Are you sure it's platform 5?" Help on hand at a temporary access near Market Street.

A place of romance

Top: Edinburgh Waverley glows like a jewel by night.

Lower left: A place of romance – as a trainee engineman, John Cameron, now the owner of this renowned locomotive the A4 BR No.60009 Union of South Africa, first met Margaret, his South African wife-to-be, at Waverley.

Centre right: The traditional Christmas tree, a feature at Waverley Station since 1945, in the concourse in 2012.

Lower right: Waverley in evening light as seen from Jacob's Ladder.

Left: Placing the last glass panel on the roof on 6 December 2012.
Below: At the roof completion event, the following were present:
from left to right, Ken Brown,(Balfour Beatty), Donald Stevenson, David Simpson, Juliet Donnachie, Paul Needham, and Alastair Barclay, (all of Network Rail) and Barry Nicol (Balfour Beatty).

Acknowledgements

To mark the refurbishment of Edinburgh Waverley, Network Rail has supported the publication of this book and special thanks are therefore due to David Simpson, Route Managing Director, Network Rail Scotland. Alistair Barclay, Project Manager, and Paul Needham, Project Scheme Manager at Waverley Station, have given welcome assistance. Juliet Donnachie, Station Manager, and Malcolm Jolly, Construction Manager, were also most helpful, as were other members of the Network Rail team. Craig Bowman, Communications Manager, offered advice and encouragement; a book about Waverley Station was his idea.

To view works in progress, Fraser Brown, Gary Cunningham, John Grady, James McAlear, Gerry McFadden and Nicola Thomson, all of Network Rail, arranged visits and are thanked for their input. For the Market Street project, Derek Barr, John Carstairs, Fergal Madden, Ian McLennan and Alan Rundell, of C.Spencer Ltd, gave much help; for the Steps project, David Storey, of Morgan Sindall Ltd, allowed regular access. Ken Brown, Senior Project Manager, Balfour Beatty Civil Engineering, and his team are also thanked for information.

The reading of the text by Hugh Begg, John Hume OBE, and John Yellowlees has been much appreciated. ScotRail generously made funding available for research and ScotRail Stations Manager John McBrinn participated in providing information.

Among others who have kindly shared their knowledge are Kenneth Blyth, Andrew Boyd, Brian Farish, Donald Cattanach, Jim Summers and Sian Yates. Many people both on and off site have taken an interest in this book. Among these are Anthony Coulson, Del Cowie, Keith Livingstone, Gregory Howard, and Craig Nelson who are thanked for their courtesy and helpfulness.

Hamish Stevenson has generously supplied images from his extensive collection while Stewart Macartney offered material from the Blyth & Blyth archives. Images have also come from David Bain, Michael Boakes, Nick Catford, Ewan Crawford, James Gildea, Tom Harden, David Hey, David Maxwell, Ian Smith and Peter Stubbs.

Staff at the National Archives of Scotland, the National Galleries of Scotland, and the National Library of Scotland are thanked for their assistance and for giving permission for the reproduction of images. The Bank of Scotland/Lloyds Bank Archives, BRB(Residuary)Ltd, the Royal Commission on Ancient and Historic Monuments of Scotland, Edinburgh Public Library, George Heriot's Trust, Glasgow City Archives, Glasgow Museums Resource Centre, Glasgow University Library, Birlinn Ltd, Ian Allan Ltd, Harper Collins Publishing, Irwell Press, The Mitchell Library and the Science & Society Picture Library at the National Railway Museum, have also made material available.

Every effort has been made to trace copyright holders of images reproduced; apologies are offered to any who have been overlooked or found untraceable.

John Peter prepared the images for publication and took the photograph for the front cover. Bruce Peter advised on book design. In Chapter 5, unless otherwise stated, the images are by the author and are her copyright.

The Balfour Beatty compound on the east concourse.

Refurbishment at Calton Road, a key access to the station.

Further Reading

C.J.A. Robertson's 'The Origins of the Scottish Railway System, 1722-1844' is a notable work. 'The North British Railway'(1975) and 'Scotland, Vol. 6,The Lowlands and the Borders' in a 'Regional History of the Railways of Great Britain' (revised 1984), both by John Thomas, have also been consulted.

In addition, 'An Illustrated History of Edinburgh's Railways' by W.A.C. Smith and Paul Anderson (1995) is insightful, as is Paul Anderson's 'Wonderful Waverley'(2003), especially for locomotive enthusiasts. Both are from Irwell Press.

Waverley Station's Refurbishment
Some Facts and Figures

Major work concerned the extensive roof where the old metal or timber was replaced with over 22.2km length of steel of various sections, giving a mass of 619 tonnes.

A work shop floor of 34.000m^2 was built and approximately 2,950 tonnes of scaffolding delivered and erected. The total surfaces shot blasted and painted amounted to approximately 50,000m^2, requiring 39,743 litres of paint. Total man/hours worked were approximately 1,250,000 hours.

For the roof's glazing, 24,700 panes of glass were installed, or 29,570m^2 with a weight of 491 tonnes. (20% was produced from recycled glass, the remainder from sustainable sources, such as sand, silicone and dolomite). For the glazing system, 316,000 fixings and 65,000 brackets were used. Total man/hours worked on glazing were 64,000.

Concourse area resurfaced: 4,000m^2
Platform resurfacing: 9,000m^2
Stone wall refurbishment: 3,000m^2
Wall cladding: 7,000m^2

Throughout the refurbishment of the station complex, recycling had a high priority:-
Concrete recycled: 93,860 tonnes
Metal recycled: 363,670 tonnes
Glass recycled: 107,620 tonnes
Timber recycled: 344,100 tonnes
Total recycled: 909,250 tonnes or 93.21%
Other waste for disposal (plastic, Perspex, asbestos cement sheets, etc) was 66,220 tonnes or 6.79%.

After refurbishment, Waverley Station has a bright, clean ambience. Here ScotRail trains are at the west side by the north ramp.